✝

INDIFFERENTISM,

OR

IS ONE RELIGION AS GOOD AS ANOTHER?

BY THE
REV. JOHN MacLAUGHLIN.

———

"*Bidendum est quis in radice cum toto orbe manserit, quis foras exierit.*"—S. OPTATUS, LIB. I. CAP. XV.

"*In radice manemus, et in toto orbe terrarum cum omnibus sumus.*"—S. OPTATUS, LIB. I. CAP. XXVIII.

45th Thousand.

LONDON: BURNS & OATES, LIMITED
LEAMINGTON AND LONDON: THE ART AND BOOK CO.
LONDON: WASHBOURNE.
LIVERPOOL: ROCKLIFF.
DUBLIN: DUFFY & CO.; GILL & SONS.
GLASGOW: MARGEY.
NEW YORK: BENZIGER BROTHERS; PUSTET & CO.
BALTIMORE: MURPHY.
MELBOURNE: ROBERTSON.

1898.

Imprimatur.

✠ CAROLUS,
Archiepiscopus Glasguen.

COMMEMORAT. S. PAULI APOSTOLI,
30 *Jun.*, 1887.

ABERDEEN UNIVERSITY PRESS.

PREFACE TO THE FORTY-FIFTH THOUSAND.

DURING the few years which have elapsed since this little book was first published, forty-five thousand copies have passed through the press.

It has spread not only through England, Ireland and Scotland, but also through the United States, Canada, Australia and India.

This circulation, which is pretty large for a book dealing with controversy, has gone much beyond the author's most sanguine anticipations.

Were it not that he is, and has been for some time, busily engaged in preparing another book —one on a kindred subject—for publication, he would be anxious to add an amount of new matter to some of the chapters.

Time does not allow him to do so at present.

Should, however, another edition be soon called for, he may see his way to introducing various points which might have the effect of making the book still more acceptable to the public.

He gladly welcomes this occasion as giving him an opportunity of tendering his warmest thanks to the editors, both Catholic and non-Catholic, who reviewed the little volume so favourably in their respective papers and periodicals. He is convinced that much of the demand which it secured even in the very early stages of its career was due to their testimonies in its behalf.

7 CUMBERLAND ROAD, ACTON, LONDON, W.,
Feast of St. Edward the Confessor, 13th Oct., 1898.

25,407

PREFACE.

IT is not without much misgiving that I offer this little book to the public. I am quite sensible of its many defects; and were it not that many friends have strongly recommended its publication, I should hardly have the courage to let it appear.

If my tiny effort, however, insignificant though it be, have no other effect except that of inducing some able and learned ecclesiastic to take up the subject, and to deal with it fully and exhaustively, I shall not deem the time I have given to it unprofitably spent.

A portion of the book consists of a development of sermons or lectures delivered—on occasions separated by long intervals—on the points of doctrine which are treated in several of the chapters. The main part of it, however, was written in what I might term "snatches" between missions; and as those missions followed each other in pretty close succession, it was seldom that I had more than a week or a fortnight of consecutive time (rarely even so much) to devote to the work of writing.

I have not aimed at style : my chief object has been to bring to the point at issue arguments which might be found solid, clear, conclusive, and convincing.

To prevent it extending beyond the intended limits, I have, in the Second Part, in which I speak of the signs and tokens of truth, treated only two of the Notes of the Church,—that is, Unity and Universality. For a similar reason I have not thought it advisable to bring out even these two in all their bearings. I have introduced *only* those features or phases of them which are *necessary* and sufficient to distinguish the one true Church from the countless false ones.

The arguments put forward apply to Christians of all denominations who believe in the inspiration of the Scriptures. Some of them may reach the position even of those who, while they do not pretend to take the Bible for their guide, nevertheless profess as much belief in a Divine revelation of some kind as saves them from the imputation of utter unbelief or extreme Rationalism.

As the title indicates, my scope is to show that all religions are not equally right, that one only can be right, that all the rest must be wrong ; and, having done this, then to point out that one which *alone* is right among the multitudinous claimants.

I cannot finish this Preface without expressing my most grateful acknowledgments to several illustrious personages and many kind and clever friends who have shown a deep interest in this tiny volume, ever since the intention of publishing it was first mentioned.

What I have written I confidently believe to be trustworthy, and in harmony with the constant teaching of the holy Catholic Church; nevertheless, I humbly and unreservedly submit everything contained in the book to the unerring judgment of the same holy Church.

Lastly, while vindicating the truth of the Catholic faith, and while disproving the claims of its antagonists and rivals, I shrink from the idea of saying anything in the tone of sarcasm, or irony, or disrespect; and I utterly disclaim all intention of indulging in personalities of any kind, even by the most distant allusions or insinuations.

JOHN MacLAUGHLIN.

11 Oak Street, Anderston, Glasgow,
Feast of the Most Holy Trinity, June 5, 1887.

CONTENTS.

PART II.

MARKS OF THE TRUE CHURCH—UNITY AND UNIVERSALITY.

CHAPTER I.

CHAPTER II.

CONCLUSION.

ON THE THRESHOLD OF THE SUBJECT.

In the following pages I propose to answer the question: " Is one religion as good as another?" In other words, I propose to discuss that popular theory which teaches that all Christian Creeds find equal favour in the eyes of God, and that it does not matter what branch of Christianity a man belongs to, provided he be a good man after his own fashion.

Lest those outside the Catholic Church, into whose hands this little book may fall, might think that, as being a Catholic priest, I have put forward my views on the subject in an exaggerated light, I wish to anticipate such charge, by quoting at the outset the words of a man whose words can evoke no such suspicion. He wrote them while he was still a Protestant, some seven or eight years before he became a Catholic. I allude to the illustrious Cardinal Newman. Long before he made up his mind to renounce Anglicanism he condemned this insidious theory in language quite as strong and emphatic as any that is used in these pages.

As early as 1838, he foresaw, with the eyes of a seer, the havoc which Indifferentism, Latitudinarianism, Liberalism in religion, would make of the Gospel, and he pointed to the gulf of unbelief to which it must inevitably lead. From the outset of his brilliant career, and while he was still a comparatively young clergyman of the Church of England, he raised his eloquent voice and wielded his powerful pen against it. He felt that those whose duty it was to try to keep down the flood of Agnosticism and infidelity must use all their energies to stem the torrent of Indifferentism. The one, he saw, was but a process of transition into the other. To *his* mind it was clear as noonday, even then, that the theory, that every man's view of revelation was equally acceptable to God, would, in the case at least of many, end in the conviction that all religions were useless.

It was to check the growth and to counteract the influence of this pernicious system that he made so many and such energetic efforts to give to the Articles of the Church of England a dogmatic interpretation— such an interpretation as would make them say something definite, and clear away from them that ambiguity which left every man free to become the arbiter of his own belief. But he was not allowed to do so.

In his *Tracts for the Times* he treats, amongst many other subjects, that of Latitudinarianism or Indifferentism. After showing that the Indifferentist or Latitudinarian may, quite consistently with his principles, deny even the fundamental doctrine of the Trinity, since that doctrine is not found on the surface of the Scriptures, he proceeds to say :—"And if the doctrine of the Trinity is not to be accounted as one of the leading or fundamental truths of revelation, the keystone of the mysterious system is lost ; and that being lost, mystery will, in matter of fact, be found gradually to fade away from the creed altogether; that is, the notion of Christianity, as being a revelation of *new truths*, will gradually fade away, and the Gospel in course of time will be considered scarcely more than a republication of the law of nature. This, I think, will be found to be the historical progress and issue of this line of thought. It is but one shape of Latitudinarianism."

In this same paper, which was published in the fifth volume in 1838, he pronounces Latitudinarianism or Indifferentism so extravagant and so unreasonable, that he declares he " cannot enter into the state of mind of a person maintaining it "—that he "conceives such a theory to be out of the question with every serious mind "—that he cannot understand " how a serious man, who realises what he is speaking about, can be a consistent Latitudinarian ". Such were his views, and such his emphatic utterances, long before he entered the Catholic Church. Time went on ; it wrought no change in him in this respect. As years rolled by, he became more and more emphatic in denouncing it. His life, as he himself has said, has been one long continuous battle against it. Well, indeed, might he say in his address, when in Rome in 1879 on the occasion of his elevation to the Cardinalate, that there was one great evil against which he had always set himself—the spirit of Liberalism or Latitudinarianism in religion.

If my space permitted, I should like to give the whole of that remarkable allocution; as it is, I can only briefly quote from it. Having thanked the Holy Father for the great honour he was conferring upon him, in raising him to the Cardinalate, he went on to say :—" And I rejoice to say, to one great mischief I have from the first opposed myself. For thirty, forty, fifty years, I have resisted to the best of my powers the spirit of Liberalism in religion. Never did the Holy Church need champions against it more sorely than now, when, alas ! it is an error overspreading as a snare the whole earth ; and on this great occasion, when it is natural for one who is in my place to look out upon the world and upon the Holy Church as it is, and upon her future, it will not, I hope, be considered out of place if I renew the protest against it which I have so often made. Liberalism in religion is the doctrine that there is no positive truth in religion, but that one creed is as good as another ; and this is the teaching which is gaining substance and force daily. It is inconsistent with the recognition of any religion as true. It teaches that all are to be tolerated, as all are matters of opinion. Revealed religion is not a truth, but a sentiment and a taste ; not an objective fact—not miraculous ; and it is the right of each individual to make it say just what strikes his fancy."

He then calls attention to the fact that it is supposed that the sects, of which Indifferentism can be said to be the only creed, constitute half the population of England. He points to the motives which the advocates of that system avow ; he describes the change which its spread has brought upon society ; and, he adds, that though in these countries it does not arise out of infidelity, it, nevertheless, ends in in-fidelity.

Such the judgment pronounced on Indifferentism by the great Cardinal, who knew so well how to de-scribe its nature, spread, influence, and effects. He had no hesitation in saying that in this country it ended in infidelity.

Now, if we look from a religious standpoint at the elements or sections which constitute the present population of England, leaving for the moment the Roman Catholic community out of sight, we can easily realise the justice of his remarks.

It is true that in one section—which includes several non-Catholic denominations—are found strict, earnest, generous, charitable Protestants, who adhere firmly to the form of religion they have inherited by family tradition, and would deem it a violation of conscience to change it for any other ; who regard the blessings of Christianity as the greatest God can bestow upon a people ; who contribute liberally to have those blessings spread among the heathen ; who advocate Christian education ; who bring up their children according to their ideas of strict social morality ; who frequent the church, read the Bible, say their prayers, encourage devotion in others, and even make vigorous efforts from time to time to increase the number of their co-religionists by winning proselytes from other denominations.

In another section, however, we find Advanced Thinkers, Agnostics, Infidels, Atheists. Whatever name they are to be called by, they no longer believe, or at least profess no longer to believe, in Christianity. They seem to have been borne away into the region of utter unbelief. And however reluctant we may be to realise the fact, this spirit of unbelief has struck its roots more deeply in these countries than many amongst us seem to imagine. It was stated in 1860, by those who were likely to have the most reliable information on the subject, that more than five millions of the population of England professed no religion of any kind. According to an official census taken about that time—alluded to in the *Times* of May the 4th, 1860—it was found that, in spite of the richest Establishment in the world—which has at least one representative in every village of the land—in Leeds and Liverpool, forty per cent. ; in Manchester, fifty-one ; in Birmingham, fifty-four ; in Lambeth, sixty-one ; and in Sheffield, sixty-two per cent., of the whole population neither had, nor professed to have, any religion whatever. "Thousands upon thousands," said an earnest advocate of the Establishment some time ago, "are living in London to whom the great truths of the Gospel are practically as little known as if the land of their birth were a heathen land, and not the great bulwark of Protestant Christianity." The rector of the important parish of St. Clement Danes, in the Strand—as reported in the *Quarterly Review* of April, 1861—said that he detected in his flock a frightful amount of infidelity—infidelity in all its shapes—extending not merely to the denying of the Christian Revelation, but even to the grossest and darkest heathenism. Another authority added : "There are whole streets within easy walk of Charing Cross, and miles and miles in more obscure places, where the people live literally without God in the world. . . . We could name entire quarters in which it seems to be the custom that men and women should live in promiscuous concubinage; where the very shopkeepers make a profession of Atheism, and encourage their poor customers to do the same." This same authority laments what he calls the well-known fact that there never was a time when the temper of the lower order was less satisfactory than it is now.

Since that time the spirit of unbelief has not been on the wane. It has never been more rampant than it is at present. The number of those who sneer at the Gospel and ridicule everything sacred, instead of getting less, is increasing every day.

Now, these two sections of the population may be looked upon as its two extreme sections. Between them there lies another, and a very large one. It consists of those who profess Christianity, but profess a form of it which is vague and variable, and as such tends to the rejection of Divine Revelation altogether.

The creed of this intermediate section of the community teaches that all religions are good—that one is practically as good as another, as all are tending towards the same end; that the great thing is to live up to them—to do what they tell us; that God is indifferent what formula of faith a man follows, provided he be a good man after his own fashion. Those who take this view of revelation hold that religion is a matter of opinion, choice, taste, sentiment, and that people may exercise their liberty as freely in choosing it as in choosing the food they eat and the clothes they wear. Or, as Cardinal Manning puts it: "People now-a-days assume that religious truth can have no definite outline and that each man must discover and define it for himself. And, however definite he may choose to be, one law is equally binding on us all. No one must be certain. Each one must concede to his neighbour as much certainty as he claims for himself. The objective certainty of truth is gone. The highest rule of certainty to each is the conviction of his own understanding. And this, in the revelation of God, and in that knowledge which is life eternal" (*The Grounds of Faith*, p. 5).

Such is the theory which is the subject of the following pages. And a most important subject it is—one which ought to be looked upon as all-important, not merely by Catholics, but also, for reasons already implied, and which we shall presently explain in detail, by strict Protestants as well.

It is the opinion of those who have the best opportunity of knowing, that Indifferentism is the chief obstacle to conversion to the Catholic faith in England. And it is the opinion of the same authorities that it is sending people in large numbers every year from Anglicanism into Agnosticism or infidelity. It may not land them there all at once, but it puts them on the road that leads there. Hence, while it is the enemy of the Catholic Church, by keeping many out of her communion, it is no less the enemy of the Protestant

Church by sweeping numbers of her children into the ranks of unbelief. In preventing them from coming to Rome, it does not, on that account, make them hold more firmly to the Anglican formularies—it rather tends to ripen them for utter infidelity. When I say it is the enemy of the Catholic Church, I do not mean that it is so from bigotry, bitter hostility, or determined opposition, for it is too tolerant of every form of belief to be sternly opposed to any. I mean it is the enemy of the Catholic Church by keeping many out of her fold. This is worth considering. There are many obstacles to England's conversion : chief amongst them is the spirit of Indifferentism, Liberalism, Latitudinarianism, or whatever name we may call it by. It stands to reason it should be so.

When a man has gone so far as to regard religion as a mere matter of opinion, and consequently as a matter of choice, he is not likely to choose a difficult one, when an easy one will suit his purpose quite as well. Naturally, men are averse to having their intellect bound down to definite doctrines, and to having their will burdened by difficult obligations. There are few, if any, who will think of embracing a creed which imposes many restraints, while they feel, or at least try to feel, they can go to heaven equally safely by one that imposes hardly any restraint at all. Why should I be asked to waste time in considering the claims of a Church which makes marriage a contract which can never, under any circumstances, be dissolved ; which binds her members to confession, to receive the Eucharist at least once a year, to assist at a certain form of worship every Sunday, to fast at stated times, to abstain on certain days from flesh-meat, to obey spiritual pastors; while I am free to remain in, or to join, a Church which imposes no obligations of the kind? As long as men are satisfied that all religions are equal in the sight of God, there is little hope of their seeking after any that differs from the easy one to which they have been accustomed.

It is quite different in the case of the strict, earnest, practical Protestant, who becomes uneasy in conscience about the truth of the creed he has hitherto professed. When *he* gets unhinged in his belief, and entertains a serious doubt as to its tenableness, he is at once involved in researches : he will inquire, read, pray; he is willing to put himself to inconvenience, and even to make sacrifices, in his anxious search after truth. But the man who enjoys unruffled peace in the wide and easy creed of Indifferentism is not likely to trouble himself with pondering on the claims of a Church which exacts stern, unchanging faith in her doctrines, and which is constantly enforcing the strict fulfilment of her precepts. Such a man will never look towards Rome except through the influence of some very special grace. And the longer he remains the adherent of a system which is only an excuse for indolence and apathy, the farther he drifts away from the definite teaching and strict discipline of the Catholic Church.

Hence, till you have banished entirely from his thoughts the conviction that one religion is as good as another, till you have cleared away from his mind the shifting sands of Indifferentism, you will not be able to lay in his understanding a foundation for definite faith. Or, as Cardinal Newman remarks, you cannot build in the aboriginal forest till you have felled the trees.

But while Indifferentism is the enemy of the Church of Rome, it is no less the enemy of the Church of England. It tends to destroy her, although it is her offspring. It has sprung from the free application of her great principle of private judgment. And the older it grows, and the larger it becomes, the more seriously does it threaten her life. Through it multitudes of her members become an easy prey to infidelity. In fact, we may say, it is a kind of preparatory school for infidelity. When men are hanging only loosely to Christianity by the elastic thread of Indifferentism, a very slight influence is sufficient to make them abandon it altogether, and leave them without faith in anything beyond the world of sense. The theory that one religion is as good as another is next neighbour to the theory that there is not much good in any religion at all. If religion is only an opinion, then every religion may be wrong, since every opinion may be wrong. And as every religion may be wrong, there is no possibility of ever arriving at any certainty about those matters religion professes to deal with : the whole thing from that moment becomes lost in impenetrable darkness. The mysteries of faith are then denied, because they appear opposed to reason ; and when the mysteries of faith are set aside, Christianity as a revelation of new and definite doctrines disappears. This state of mind gradually prepares a man for the wholesale denial of Christianity as a Divine Revelation ; and hence the step from Indifferentism into utter unbelief is natural and easy.

But let us come from the abstract to the concrete, from possibilities to things which are taking place in actual life under our own eyes. See what is going on in our midst. It is no secret that the rapid growth of unbelief, chiefly among persons of education, is mainly due to the fact that the ceaseless divisions in the various branches of Anglicanism have generated in the minds of many the conviction that Christianity is a failure. Numbers of men, formerly Protestants, and, for the most part, men of cultivated intellect, have declared that they have ceased to believe in Christian revelation altogether, in consequence of the Church of England tolerating within her pale absolutely contradictory teaching on the most fundamental doctrines of the Christian creed. Such men could never reconcile themselves to the view that that Church was, as she professed to be, a Divine Teacher, when she approved totally opposite views of the religion of which she was the recognised organ.

Now when people of non-Catholic denominations thus lose all confidence in the religion they have hitherto professed, they do not, as a rule, look, or care to look, in any other direction for consistency and truth. They find no book, or at all events they *read* no book, which would have the effect of turning their thoughts towards that one sanctuary of truth, that everlasting treasure-house, in which alone are found harmonious unity, unchanging doctrine, perfect consistency, everything that can satisfy the cravings of the human mind—that is, the Catholic Church.

On the other hand, the infidel literature of the day, which is pouring from the press like a deluge, and which threatens to submerge the greater part of the earth, easily finds its way into their hands. It preaches a new gospel—one just suited to their present temper of mind; it pronounces Christianity a myth, a fable, an antiquated superstition, a bundle of conflicting doctrines which cannot bear the test of scientific investigation; its shallow blasphemous arguments are clothed in that elegant sophistry which its ingenious propagandists know so well how to use. These arguments meet with hardly any resistance in the mind of the Christian Indifferentist who has no definite form of belief to cling to. He has seen nothing but contradiction in the creed he has been accustomed to, and he is captivated by the apparently more consistent principles of infidelity. He becomes its disciple. He gives himself up unreservedly to its teaching; and he does so all the more willingly, because, while his late Christian profession imposed upon him some semblance of moral restraint, infidelity relieves him of restraint altogether. He is no longer crippled by the pains of conscience. He becomes dead to all sense of moral responsibility. He can go where inclination leads, give loose reins to his passions, gratify every desire with impunity; for while he hopes for no future reward, he fears no future punishment.

Indifferentism, then, Liberalism in religion, Latitudinarianism, acted on by the infidel press of the day, is sending thousands of members every year from the Establishment into Atheism. It is sapping her very foundations. Hence, to say the least, Protestants have as much reason to hate it as Catholics have. The injury it inflicts on Protestantism is greater than the injury it inflicts on Catholicity. The one is negative, the other positive. While it only tends to put farther and farther away from the Church of Rome people who never belonged to her, and renders them less disposed to examine into her claims, it, on the other hand, robs the Establishment of multitudes of her baptised members and consigns them to hopeless unbelief. This it has been doing, this it is doing still, this it will continue to do. And the end will be, says a writer of this generation, that it will sweep so many from her ranks into the region of the "Unknowable," that whenever the State withdraws its sustaining hand, as soon as those props and buttresses, by which the civil power keeps her standing, give way, she will totter and fall to pieces ; and in the day of her downfall there will be few sincere adherents remaining to weep over her dissolution.

Bossuet foresaw this, and predicted it. Speaking of the great revolt of the sixteenth century, and referring specially to England, he says : "Every man erects a tribunal for himself, where he becomes the arbiter of his own belief. Although the innovators wished to restrain the minds of men within the limits of Holy Scripture, yet as each individual was constituted its interpreter, and was to believe that the Holy Scripture would discover to him its meaning, all were authorised to worship their own inventions, to consecrate their own errors, and to place the seal of the Divinity on their own thoughts. It was then foreseen that by this unbridled licence sects would be multiplied to infinity, and that while some would not cease to dispute or to hold their reveries for inspirations, others, wearied by visions of folly, and not able to recognise the majesty of religion, torn asunder by so many sects, would seek at length a fatal repose and complete independence in indifference to all religion, or Atheism."

Dr. Moriarty, lately Bishop of Kerry, who, in his allocution to his clergy on " The Church Establishment," quotes the above passage, adds: " Why was not the latter part of this prophecy sooner and more universally fulfilled amongst us ? What was it that retarded the erring mind in its downward path towards infidelity ? While Protestantism elsewhere rapidly changed into Rationalism, in these countries it even yet retains a large portion of Christian truth. The material and golden bond of an endowed Establishment furnishes the only reasonable explanation we can suggest for standing still upon the steep incline. Besides the rewards offered to orthodoxy, its connection with the State preserved while it enslaved it ; the dry, hard, unyielding discipline of law and government insisted on the observance of forms and formularies, and thus kept Protestantism in shape, as bodies though lifeless are preserved in ice."

We have seen that Cardinal Newman considers this pernicious theory to be the religion of half the population of England. Any one who has mixed much with the masses, and who has seen how widely it is spread, and the hold it has taken on the mind of the multitude, must feel that his estimate is not beyond the mark. The popularity it has attained in all classes of society is astounding. It may be justly named the most popular creed of the day. In mixing with people of non-Catholic denominations in the large towns and country districts of England, I have frequently asked persons who were not Catholics (but whose Catholic connections desired me to put the question) whether they had any objection to become members of the Roman Catholic communion. On most occasions the answers I received indicated clearly enough that this flexible system of Indifferentism was their only creed. They spoke as if they were perfectly satisfied with it, and seemed to have no appetite for anything in the shape of religion beyond it.

Repeatedly I have heard candid, straightforward professions like the following : " I cannot say that I have any objection to the Roman Catholic religion ; " " One religion is as good as another ; " " All religions are good ; " " It makes no matter what we are when we are Christians at all ". Avowals such as these made it clear to evidence that the persons from whom they came had no idea of the necessity of belonging to any one definite Christian creed, or of holding fast to any special doctrine of revelation. They spoke as if they might choose a religion to-day and change it to-morrow, and change the one of to-morrow for a widely different one the day following, and repeat these changes until they had gone round the whole circle of Christian sects ; and as if they might do all this without imperilling their salvation in any way whatever, at least so far as forms of belief were concerned.

But with all this I perceived signs of great docility, a praiseworthy willingness to reason, to compare claims, to listen to the Catholic view of the question, to listen even to an explanation of the uncompromising attitude of the Catholic Church with regard to her symbol of faith. In many instances I have had an opportunity of speaking a second and a third time, and several times successively, to those who in the first interview expressed their convictions in the language to which I have referred. And, as a rule, I may say, when I showed them the unreasonableness and untenableness of their theory, and proved to them that one, and *only* one, religion could be true, that all the others must be false, that those who had a serious doubt whether they belonged to the true one or not were bound to strive to find a solution of their doubt, they seemed to have an incipient want of confidence in Indifferentism as a creed, were quite willing to make researches, to receive instruction, and eagerly anxious to have their doubts removed. I may add that as their honest inquiry was accompanied by humble and persevering prayer for light, it ended almost invariably in their submission to the Catholic Church.

It was this experience that suggested to me the idea of publishing what the following pages contain. When I perceived, on the one hand, that this broad, undefined Christianity, or Indifferentism in religion, had become the creed of so large a proportion amongst the masses; and when I perceived, on the other hand, on the part of so many (in fact, nearly all with whom I came in contact), a willingness to inquire, an eagerness to receive instruction, it occurred to me that it would be worth while to strive to make reach the multitude, in a pamphlet or small book, those popular and familiar, but at the same time forcible, arguments which a priest would use with such class of persons if he spoke to them separately and individually on this phase of religion.

I knew well from the outset that the undertaking was beset by numberless difficulties. Something of the kind could be easily enough written; but how get it into the hands of those for whom it was chiefly intended?

This was the difficulty that almost deterred me from making the attempt, and this is my difficulty still. The very fact that a book is written by a Catholic priest, and that the book deals with matters of controversy, is sufficient to prejudice those outside the Catholic Church against it. Many are so opposed, through bigotry, education, associations, surroundings, to what they consider the narrowness, exclusiveness, and arrogant attitude of the Church of Rome, and are so captivated by that broad and wide creed which is so tolerant of other people's views, so benevolent, so aptly designed to make allowances for country, character, dispositions, circumstances, that they are afraid to read any book, and are not at all likely to *buy* any book, which might have the effect of upsetting their present comfortable convictions.

This certainly is a difficulty, and a serious one. So, as far as getting expositions of Catholic doctrine directly spread amongst the non-Catholic population is concerned, we are powerless. Hitherto the Protestant masses have marshalled themselves in such serried ranks against what has been termed Popish aggressiveness, that it has been impossible for any Catholic missive to penetrate them. They have been like a wall of brass, impervious to every Catholic effort.

This is one of the great disadvantages under which the Catholic Church has been labouring in England. Of the many splendid developments, expositions, vindications, apologies, of Catholic doctrine which have been written in England (compared with any of which this little tract dwindles into insignificance), comparatively few have reached the non-Catholic multitude. The persistent traditional horror of religious interference, and the particular dread of anything that savoured of Popery, has been one of the chief obstacles. And it may be thought that the difficulty will be exceptionally great with regard to the present little book, since it bears a rather significant title, and since many people have already made up their minds once for all that the creed which teaches that one religion is as good as another is the easiest, the most convenient, the most agreeable, and, as far as they can see, quite as safe as any other.

It would be a step in the right direction if we could succeed in concentrating the mind of the multitude on the statement that all religions cannot be right, that one only can be right, and that all the rest must be wrong; and that, in case of rational doubt about one's present position, it is necessary to inquire, to search after a solution of the doubt.

Happily there has been a great advance towards the Catholic Church since the early part of this century. Although the happy change of feeling has not reached the extent earnest Catholics could have desired, yet it has been wider and deeper than many had anticipated. Numerous and honoured are the names of those who have sacrificed everything in their noble pursuit after truth—have abjured sectarianism, have broken the fondest and firmest family ties, and have been enrolled as members of the Roman Catholic communion. From the steps of the throne down to the street-sweeper, the work of conversion has been steadily going on. Nobles, clergymen, lawyers, physicians, trades people, working people, have seen the error of their hereditary faith, and have generously renounced it to embrace another. And not merely have men of noble rank and of great parts, at extreme personal inconvenience, embraced Catholicism, but even ladies of great intellectual power and rare accomplishments have not shrunk from sacrifices which one would have thought would have appalled their sex, when sincere and unprejudiced inquiry made it clear to them which was the one true religion amongst the numberless claimants.

The natural result of these many conversions has been the gradual decline of that spirit of bitter hostility which actuated almost the whole public mind of England as late as the first part of this century. It is no longer the fashion to say what, we are told, it was quite fashionable to say some sixty or seventy years ago—" All Papists must be damned, just because they are Papists ". No ; most of our dissenting brethren will grant that people may be saved in the Catholic religion as easily as in any other. Some, who are more liberal in their admissions, will grant that the Catholic religion was the first religion of Christianity and is most likely to be the last ; and that, as far as they can see, it is the holiest, and ought therefore to be the safest. When they have begun to see things in this light, instruction and earnest prayer will easily complete the good work—*i.e.*, impel them to take the final step which will bring them safely into the bosom of the one true Church.

While I mean this little book chiefly for those outside the Church, I mean it also for some who are within. There are Catholics who are disposed to make concessions which their Church can never warrant. They move in a circle of society, or are placed in circumstances, where they are strongly tempted to temporise in matters of religion. They may be inclined to attach much more importance to expediency, or to certain false notions of etiquette, than to duty even of a sacred kind. For example, they hear it stated in some drawing-room assembly, or at some nobleman's dining-table, where the tone of the conversation is notably Protestant, that, after all, one religion is quite as good as another — that there is hardly any difference of any importance, that it is

quite immaterial what creed a man follows, provided
he be an honest man, pay twenty shillings in the
pound, do no injury to his neighbour in his property
or in his character, and discharge his duty faithfully
as a benevolent member of society. Now, if they
(Catholics) chime in with this liberal doctrine, endorse
it, express assent to it, or imply assent to it, they are
simply encouraging heresy, virtually propagating it,
sacrificing their most sacred convictions to erroneous
ideas of politeness—or rather, allowing themselves to
be swayed by the lowest and most despicable form of
human respect. They imagine, perhaps, that by this
kind of liberalistic spirit they will find favour in the
eyes of those who are above them in social position.
It is just the contrary. Even the very persons, to
gain or to retain whose esteem they thus make admissions which their Church and their own conscience
condemn, will soon begin to look on them with contempt and distrust. The Catholic Church cannot
tolerate any compromise. She is not at liberty to
allow even the least morsel of error to be mixed up
with the sacred deposit of truth which has been en-
trusted to her.

And hence she can never countenance the low,
grovelling complaisance of those who seek to further
their own interests by expressing their approbation of
statements which are entirely at variance with her
teachings. Of course, I do not mean that the Catholic
faithful ought to be eager to engage in controversy,
to be uselessly parading their faith, or to be obtruding
it in an offensive manner upon others; but I *do* mean

that it is altogether unlawful (for them) to sanction, either explicitly or implicitly, a system of religion which embodies the most subtle, popular, and dangerous heresy of the present day—*i.e.*, that broad and wide Christianity which teaches that all religions find equal favour in the eyes of God.

" In private life," says Cardinal Manning, "we ought to be kindly and unobtrusive, but uncompromising in confessing our Faith ; never forcing it upon the unwilling, but never silent when we ought to speak " (*Sermon on Indifference*, Advent, 1884).

PART FIRST.

CHAPTER I.

Refutation of Indifferentism from Reason, and from Reason enlightened by Faith.

ONE of the most popular, plausible, and at the same time one of the most pernicious theories about religion at the present day is the theory which teaches that a man may be quite indifferent to what Christian creed he belongs, provided he be a good man after his own fashion. This theory may be called by some Latitudinarianism, by others Liberalism in religion, by others, again, Indifferentism. Whatever name we give it, it means simply the doctrine that one religion is as good as another, or that all creeds are equally agreeable in the eyes of God. Its advocates say, and say in the plainest terms, that God does not care what religion His creatures profess, provided they live up to and act consistently with the one which they have embraced, or the one which has been handed down to them by family tradition. They contend, in fact, that men may claim as large a measure of liberty in choosing the creed they profess as in choosing their place of residence or their family doctor. Instead of making religious belief a matter of duty, they, on the contrary, make it a matter of choice, taste, sentiment, and inclination. They act and speak and think, or at least affect to think, that while God holds up, as it were, before men's minds certain doctrines which He commands to be believed, men are, nevertheless, free to put aside those doctrines and to choose other doctrines, *even contradictory ones*, in their stead. Their reasoning, when analysed, must force them inevitably to the conclusion that, although the voice of the God of everlasting truth has declared something to be true, they are at liberty to believe it to be false ; and that while that same unerring voice proclaims some statement to be false, they, in the enjoyment of the fulness of their right of private judgment, are free to look upon it as true. Liberty of choice with regard to forms of Christian belief means nothing less than this.

Does this theory, which eloquent sophistry has made so plausible, deserve the popularity which it has attained, and which has given it such a hold on the mind of the multitude ? No ; so far from deserving the approbation, it does not deserve even the toleration of any reasonable man. Let us weigh it in the balance of truth. Let us look at it in the light of right reason and of Divine revelation, and we shall find that it contradicts at once man's reason and God's revelation.

In this chapter we shall deal with it as a contradiction of reason.

God being what He is, that is, the God of eternal truth, He cannot be indifferent as to whether His people believe this particular creed or some other creed that contradicts it. To say that He does not care what form of Christianity they profess is exactly equivalent to saying that He does not care whether they believe what is true or what is false. For the different creeds which now exist, and which, all of them, press their claim on the homage of man's mind, contradict each other ; and contradict each other not merely in small items of belief, but even in doctrines which are commonly looked upon as fundamental by those belonging to any Christian denomination. One Church teaches that Christ is truly, really, and substantially present in the sacrament of the Eucharist ; another Church teaches that He is *not* truly present in the sacrament of the Eucharist. One Church teaches that the priest has power to forgive the grievous sins committed after baptism ; another Church teaches that the priest has *not* power to forgive the grievous sins committed after baptism. One Church holds that the Pope has universal spiritual jurisdiction over the whole world, and that his utterances are infallible when he speaks on faith and morals in certain given circumstances ; other Churches maintain that the Pope has *not* universal spiritual jurisdiction over the whole world, and that his utterances are *not* infallible in those circumstances in which members of the Roman Catholic communion say they are infallible.

Now, here are statements, and here are contradictory statements, and contradictory statements in matters of great moment—in doctrines which touch even the very foundations of faith. The voice of reason is peremptory and emphatic. It proclaims, in a tone that cannot be mistaken, that the creed which affirms these propositions, and the creed which denies them, cannot be both true. Two statements that contradict each other cannot both be true at once. One only can be true, the other must be false; and the evident truth of one establishes the evident falsehood of the other. To say, therefore, that God does not care whether His people profess this religion or that other religion which is in contradictory opposition to it, is exactly the same as to say that He does not care whether they believe truth or falsehood.

Now, philosophy (which is a science of reason) demonstrates that veracity, or essential truthfulness, is one of God's attributes. In virtue of this essential attribute, God not only loves truth, but loves truth of necessity; and not only hates falsehood, but must, as a law of His being, bear an undying, an eternal hatred to it. And hence, to affirm that He leaves people free to believe what is true or what is false, as they choose, is nothing short of a blasphemy against His attribute of essential truthfulness. The moment we affirm that one religion is as good as another, and that it is a matter of indifference with God what form of Christian belief men adopt, that moment we are hurried in_evitably into the blasphemous conclusion that He is not more glorified by the profession of the doctrines which He Himself has revealed, than He is by the profession of those false theories of men which contradict them. If *He* has condescended to reveal from on high one definite religion (and all professing Christians freely admit that He has done so), surely He cannot be indifferent whether that one definite religion which He has thus revealed be believed, or some other religion which is in open, palpable opposition to it.

This statement, which is clear enough in its bare enunciation, will become still more clear in the light of the following illustrations. We read in the Old Testament that when the Israelites, in their journey through the desert, had reached the wilderness of Sinai, having the mountain of Sinai over against them, the time was come when God was to make known the Ten Commandments, and to have a tabernacle and an ark constructed for His worship. It was on that memorable occasion He revealed to Moses the precise plan according to which both tabernacle and ark were to be made. He was not content with describing the general dimensions, such as the length, the breadth, the height : He went down to the most minute details. He specified the particular kind of wood of which both were to be made—*i.e.*, Setim wood. He specified also the particular way in which they were to be overlaid with gold ; and He added the other precious materials which were to be used in their decoration. No human architect could enter more minutely into details, in giving a design for some earthly structure, than the great Divine Architect did on that occasion, when there was question of giving the plan after which His ark and tabernacle were to be fashioned. And if He was so explicit in the directions He gave, it was simply because He meant to show that He would not leave any room for the promptings of man's imagination, fancy, or private judgment in the construction of those sacred appurtenances for His worship. Hence, he charged Moses, in words on which He laid all the emphasis His Divine Voice could command, to keep to and not to depart in the least item from the plan which had been revealed to him. "Look," He said, "and make it" (the ark) "according to the pattern which was shown thee in the mount" (*Exod.* xxv. 40).

Now let us suppose that as soon as Moses had gone down from the mountain, he had begun to make the tabernacle and the ark, *not* according to the plan which had been divinely revealed to him, but according to a plan struck out of his own head, would God have sanctioned the change? If he (Moses) had departed from the pattern thus divinely shown to him, and shown to him in such minute, precise, definite detail, and had constructed tabernacle and ark according to the dictates of his own private judgment, God would not have recognised either as the thing which He had commanded to be made. And surely we cannot say that the God of infinite knowledge, of infinite wisdom, of eternal truth, is more concerned about the length and breadth of a material thing than about those momentous truths which go to build up the noble, majestic structure of His religion.

The intercourse of Moses with God on the mountain furnishes us with another illustration which is quite as much to the point. It directs our thoughts in the same channel. It was there that God gave to him, written with His own finger on tables of stone, those Ten Commandments which were to form the basis of

all moral law. He directed him to make these Commandments known to the people. Such was the
commission given to Moses, and such the message he
was to announce. His work was marked out for him.
He was not the maker of the law; he was but the
vehicle by which it was to pass to the people. When
he received those binding precepts from the hands of
that great Sovereign Lord and Creator to whom man
owed both the homage of the mind and the service of
the body, he was not at liberty to put them aside, and
give to the people precepts of his own making. He
had no power to change the law, of which those precepts were the expression. He could not add to it;
he could not take away from it. He was bound to
give it to the people as he himself received it, in all its
purity, integrity, and definiteness. On the other hand,
similar obligations rested on the people as soon as the
promulgation of those precepts reached them. When
they heard them from the lips of Moses, who announced them in the name of God, whose representative he was, they were not free to depart from them,
and to frame for themselves other precepts which
would be more in harmony with their natural inclinations. No; there was the Divine code, there the
expression of God's law for man, clear, distinct,
definite; and man was bound to follow it, and for-
bidden to follow any that was at variance with it.

Now, Moses appeared in the Old Dispensation as the
oracle of Divine Truth to those of whom he was the
chief, as the medium of that partial revelation which
God then vouchsafed to make to His people.

Jesus Christ appeared in the New Dispensation, when the fulness of time was come, to reveal additional doctrines to the world—doctrines immeasurably more important. And if those who lived in the centuries which intervened between the days of Moses and the Incarnation were obliged to adhere to the portion of revelation made to them through the lips of that Great Lawgiver, surely the people of the present Dispensation are as strictly obliged to embrace and adhere to that religion, when it has been enlarged, completed, and perfected by God's own Incarnate Son, who is the Way, the Truth, and the Life.

The foregoing arguments may be summed up in these two sentences: 1st, Right reason can never sanction contradiction, and, therefore, can never sanction Indifferentism; 2nd, If God does not allow any change to be made in the plan He gives for the construction of a material sanctuary for His worship, it is against all reason to hold that He will allow any change to be made in the doctrines which teach in what His true worship consists—that is, in the truths He wishes to be believed and the laws He wishes to be fulfilled.

———

CHAPTER II.

Refutation of Indifferentism from Revelation—Indifferentism a Contradiction of Revelation.

THIS theory of Indifferentism is also a contradiction of Revelation. After His resurrection from the dead,

and before He ascended to His Father, our Divine
Lord appeared on a mountain in Galilee. His Apostles
were there to meet Him. His appearing on that particular mountain had been expected ; it had been
previously announced by Himself. It was natural it
should be a meeting of special appointment. It was
one of unequalled import. Its results were to sway
the world to the end of time. The interests of the
whole human race would be influenced by it.

It was there our Divine Lord gave to His Apostles
that great commission to which the world owes its
conversion. " Going," He said to them, " teach ye
all nations, baptising them in the name of the Father,
and of the Son, and of the Holy Ghost. Teaching
them to observe all things whatsoever I have commanded you. And behold I am with you all days,
even to the consummation of the world" (*Matt.* xxviii.
19, 20).

" Teach ye all nations," He said. What were they
to teach ? They were to teach the truths of His faith
and the precepts of His law. And they were to teach
all nations these self-same truths and precepts. He
could not mean that, when they divided the earth into
those vast districts which were to be the spheres of
their respective apostolates, one Apostle was to preach
in one country that there was a sacrament in the
Church by which the sins committed after baptism
could be forgiven, and that another Apostle was to
preach in another country that there was no such
sacrament. He could not mean either, when He thus
sent them forth in His name, that He authorised some

amongst them to announce that He was truly and really and substantially present in the sacrament of the Eucharist, and that He authorised others of them to preach the contradictory—*i.e.*, that He was *not* truly present in that sacrament. No; He left no room for the play of fancy, or the promptings of imagination, or the dictates of private judgment. He would have them understand—and understand beyond all manner of doubt—that as He was the One Only God, so there could be only one true religion which was the faithful expression of His Divine mind to His people. Being the God of essential truthfulness, He would not allow man's error to be mixed up with His truth. He would permit no human authority to add to His doctrines; nor would He permit any human authority to diminish them.

Mark well the words He added, with such significance and such emphasis, when He gave His Apostles the great world-wide commission to teach. They call for special notice; for we must remember that they were sounded by that same Omnipotent Voice which spoke to Moses on Sinai, when the great commission of promulgating the Ten Commandments was given him, and when the plan of the ark and of the tabernacle was shown him; and when God said to him: "Look and make it after the pattern that was shown thee on the mount". We must remember, too, that the Apostles and their successors had as little power to change the doctrines they were then commissioned to preach as Moses had to change the Ten Commandments, or to change the plan according to which the ark and the tabernacle were to be constructed. The words in question prove this to evidence. "Teaching them," He said, "to observe ALL things whatsoever I have commanded you." He did not say, Teaching them to observe this portion of what I have commanded you; nor did He say, Teaching them to observe that other portion of what I have commanded you; but He said, "Teaching them to observe ALL *things whatsoever* I have commanded you". "All things," whether in the domain of faith or in the domain of morals.

It was as if He had said, You are not to teach them that they may observe whatever they will take into their heads to observe, or whatever their individual preference or private judgment may dictate; nor are you to teach them that they may observe whatever *your* own private judgment dictates or *your* imagination prompts; but you are to teach them to observe all things whatsoever I have commanded you—these things and nothing else. You are to make them feel that they have no liberty of choice, that I will never tolerate the innovations of human opinion upon the doctrines which, through My Church, I teach, or upon the laws which, through her, I enforce.

May we not say that these words, "Teaching them to observe all things whatsoever I have commanded you," without straining them in the least, without stretching them beyond their natural obvious import, are equivalent to a positive, absolute condemnation of the theory of Indifferentism? For, did not these words mean something definite and certain in the mind of our Lord; did He not intend them to mean some thing definite and certain in the minds of His Apostles; and did He not intend *by* them to empower and oblige His Apostles to convey that definite and certain "something" to the nations which they were to teach? But the argument gathers additional strength from the fact that when our Lord gave to His Apostles this great world-wide commission to teach, He knew well how much it would cost them to carry it out. Being God as well as man, the future lay as clear before Him as the past and the then present. The stern, desperate opposition they must meet with—the sufferings, the humiliations, the privations they must endure in their long, laborious career, were all present to His mind when He spoke the words, "Going, teach all nations". He saw their scourgings, the prisons in which they would be chained, the days and nights they must pass in hunger, thirst, and cold. He saw, too, the violent deaths that were in store for them. And He saw all these things not in vague outline, but in all their terrible, revolting, and harrowing details. He saw the shipwrecks, the imprisonments, the cauldron of boiling oil, the flaying alive, the beheading, the crucifixion with head downwards. He knew well that their lives were to be lives of unceasing toil, pain, and contempt, and that their deaths were to be the deaths of malefactors.

Yet these men were His own chosen ones. They were His dearest friends; they were the men nearly all of whom had been with Him throughout His public life—the men whom He loved with the fondest love of His sacred, loving Heart.

But how reconcile the love He bore them, and His clear foreknowledge of their life-long martyrdom, with the statement that He is quite indifferent what faith people hold, provided they act consistently with it? Would it not have been cruel on His part thus to doom His special servants, His dearest friends, to those lives of suffering and deaths of shame, if it was a matter of no consequence to Him whether His people worshipped Him according to this creed or that? If men, by acting consistently with whatever idea of religion they already held, became sufficiently acceptable to Him, why not leave them as they were, and save the Apostles from such trials in life and such torments in death?

Let them act up to the lights of nature—those lights gave them a certain notion of religion; that notion of it, though full of error, was for them as good as any other (according to the principles of our opponents) if their life was in harmony with it. Or, in case some fragment of definite positive revelation, through intercourse with the Jews, or through the promulgation of Christianity at Jerusalem, by chance reached them, let them use it according to casual or ordinary helps, and let further illumination, if deemed expedient, for some particularly privileged soul (like Cornelius) be vouchsafed by the ministry of an angel. But why condemn an Apostle to a life of incessant pain and a death of unheard-of torment in order to bring to his fellow-man a message of salvation, if his fellow-man was free (in spite of every evidence of its truth) to accept that message or to reject it, or to accept a part and reject the rest, and could make himself quite as agreeable to God *without* it as *with* it? Does not the fact of His giving that great commission to His Apostles prove that He meant them to convey to His people some definite message of revelation which His people could not know by any natural means? And does not His foresight of the storms of persecution they were to encounter, and the tremendous trials they were to undergo, show how extremely important He considered it that that message should reach them? Who can give *us* permission to treat as insignificant, or to be indifferent about, a message, or the true meaning of a message, to which a God of infinite wisdom attached so much importance? None but Himself could give such permission, and He could not do so without defeating His own ends.

I can easily anticipate the argument that will spring to the lips of Indifferentists in answer to this reasoning. It is in vain, however, for them to urge it. The very comprehensiveness of their system makes it powerless. They say that the Apostles were sent to teach and to preach, in order that men might know and believe in Christ, the Mediator, whose mediation or redemption was the leading idea, or the great fundamental truth, of the Gospel—a truth which men could not know by the light of reason, or by any revelation made heretofore to the Jews.

But the very men who say this comprise in their theory of liberal religion Socinians and Unitarians, who do not believe in the Divinity of Christ at all—do

not believe in original sin—do not believe in Redemption—who reject all the mysteries of religion,
from the very fact that they *are* mysteries, and that,
therefore, reason cannot comprehend them. I mean,
they will tell us that the Socinian or Unitarian, who
acts up to what his religion teaches, can quite as easily
find favour in the eyes of God, and therefore quite as
easily save his soul, as the man who professes the
most detailed and most complete form of Christian
belief; and that it is a matter of indifference to God
whether a man chooses for his creed Unitarianism
pure and simple, which absolutely denies the mystery
of Redemption, or chooses some other formula of
religion which emphatically affirms that mystery as one
of the most vital doctrines of Christianity.

The conclusion from such premises is clear; it
must be this. Therefore it was quite useless to put
the Apostles to such trouble, to force them to lead a
life of perpetual self-sacrifice, in announcing the doctrine of Redemption, since men, though living in a
country where that doctrine is widely professed, clearly
explained, sustained by sound and convincing proofs
are free to form and cling to a creed from which it is
sedulously excluded; and while exercising such wide
liberty in the choice of a creed, are doing an act which
in itself is quite as acceptable in the eyes of God, and
quite as apt to promote salvation, as would be the act
of faith made by him whose creed contains with absolute certainty all those doctrines our Lord referred to
when He said to His Apostles: "Teaching them to
observe all things whatsoever I have commanded you".

But there is another answer to this sophistry. On what grounds does the Indifferentist, or Latitudinarian, or advocate of any form of liberal religion single out the mystery of Redemption, or any other isolated doctrine of Christianity, as *the* one for the promulgation of which *principally* the Apostles were to traverse the earth, spend their lives in toil, shed their blood, and die the martyr's death? Were not those Apostles as strictly bound to announce all the doctrines which that Redeemer taught as they were to announce the truth that HE was the Redeemer? Is not this evident from the words He Himself made use of when He gave them the world-wide commission: "Teaching them to observe *all* things whatsoever I have commanded you"? Was there anything in that commission, either expressed or understood, to warrant them in believing that He gave them leave to class His doctrines under the heads of principal and subordinate, or to put forward some as of primary and others as of secondary importance? Did they not look upon everything that came from His lips as equally important and equally grave? Did they claim to have any share in formulating the creed they were to teach by choosing some of His precepts and rejecting others? Did they not know that to reject one iota of His revelation was to deny His authority altogether? And did not the same reasons which bound the people who were taught by the Apostles to believe some of the Gospel truths bind them to believe *all* the Gospel truths? What reason could there be for receiving part and for rejecting the rest? Why believe the Apostles credible up to a certain point and look upon them as totally unworthy of credence beyond that point? But, above all, why should the Apostles be sent to preach at all, if it mattered so little whether men believed or did not believe even those doctrines which are looked upon by most Christians as the leading fundamental doctrines of the Gospel? Must not then the preaching of the Apostles (in the theory of our opponents) be regarded as vain and meaningless?

Cardinal Newman, in his book entitled *Discussions and Arguments*, traces the sad issue to which this "marking out" or "singling out" of favourite doctrines leads. "Many," he says, "would fain discern one or two doctrines in the Scripture clearly, and no more; or some generalised form, yet not so much as a body of doctrine of any character. They consider that a certain message, consisting of one or two great and simple statements, makes up the whole of the Gospel, and that these are plainly in the Scriptures: accordingly, that he who holds and acts upon these is a Christian, and ought to be acknowledged by all to be such, for in holding these he holds all that is necessary. These statements they sometimes call the essentials, the peculiar doctrines, the leading ideas, the vital doctrines, the great truths of the Gospel; and all this sounds very well; but when we come to realise what is abstractedly so plausible, we are met by this insuperable difficulty, that no great number of persons agree together what are those great truths, simple views, leading ideas, or peculiar doctrines of the

Gospel. Some say that the doctrine of the Atone-
ment is the leading idea; some the doctrine of
spiritual influence; some that both together are the
peculiar doctrines; some that love is all in all; some
that the acknowledgment that Jesus is the Christ, and
some that the resurrection from the dead; some that
the announcement of the soul's immortality is, after
all, the essence of the Gospel, and all that need be
believed."

Then, in the words which he subjoins, and which
we have already quoted in page 10, he shows that the
Indifferentist, following out his principles of latitude,
may, without any inconsistency, deny even the dogma
of the Trinity; and that if that great fundamental
mystery is put aside, mystery gradually disappears
from the Christian creed altogether. He observes also
that the Gospel under the destructive influence of
Indifferentism becomes merely an equivalent for a
new publication of the law of Nature. In other words,
the Indifferentist, who believes himself a Christian
because he professes this broad, undefined Christianity, is pretty much on a level with those who are
entirely outside the pale of Christendom, whom no
ray of revealed religion has ever yet reached—that
is, as far as Divine faith is concerned, he is on a level
with such. As to salvation, it may be said that his
chances of being saved are less, since he rejects lights
which to the heathen were never offered—unless,
indeed, he be one of those in whose case good faith
or invincible ignorance may plead in their behalf.

The inevitable results to which Latitudinarianism

4

Indifferentism, Liberalism in religion, leads, could not be more beautifully or more accurately described than in the words of the great Cardinal which I have quoted, and which were written by him several years before he became a Catholic. To hold that every man's view of revealed religion is acceptable to God, if he acts up to it, that no one view is in itself better than another, is simply to reduce Christianity to a level with natural morality—to lead men on gradually, though it may be slowly, to the gulf of absolute unbelief. Now if a theory, the natural tendency of which is to lead to such lamentable consequences, is maintainable, then the preaching of the Gospel on the part of the Apostles, at the expense of health, happiness and life, was a work useless and foolish in the extreme. And if it was useless and foolish on the part of the Apostles to suffer so much in preaching the New Revelation, it was equally useless and foolish on the part of those faithful who have endured martyrdom to suffer so much in professing and practising what it taught. Why so many thousands living in the Catacombs, why so many thrown to wild beasts in the amphitheatre, why so many, throughout the history of the Church, imprisoned for life, burned or beheaded, hanged and quartered? Why might not these heroic souls have chosen some easy form of religion that would have saved them from such tremendous sacrifices, rather than that detailed, stern, inflexible one which cost them the loss of earthly goods, earthly happiness, and even their blood and their life?

CHAPTER III.

Indifferentism shown to be a Contradiction of Revelation from the history of Cornelius the Centurion.

THE tenth chapter of the Acts of the Apostles gives the narrative of a conversion of a man whose conversion may be regarded as an unanswerable refutation of the theory of Indifferentism. I refer to the conversion of Cornelius the Centurion.

The virtues this man practised before St. Peter saw him, the stern uprightness with which he had acted up to the lights hitherto received, the succession of miraculous circumstances which led to his conversion, make it clear to evidence that indifference in matters

---

* Now there was a certain man in Cesarea named Cornelius, a centurion of the band which is called the Italian. 2. A religious man, and one that feared God with all his house, who gave much alms to the people, and prayed to God always. 3. He saw in a vision manifestly, about the ninth hour of the day, an angel of God coming unto him, and saying to him: Cornelius. 4. And he, beholding him, being seized with fear, said: What is it, Lord? And he said to him: Thy prayers and thy alms have ascended for a memorial in the sight of God. 5. And now send men to Joppe, and call hither one Simon, who is surnamed Peter: 6. He lodgeth with one Simon a tanner, whose house is by the sea-side: he shall tell thee what thou must do. 7. And when the angel who spoke to him was departed, he called two of his household servants, and a soldier that feared the Lord, of those who were under him: 8. To whom when he had related all, he sent them to Joppe. 9. And on the next day, whilst they were going on their journey, and drawing near to the city, Peter went up to the higher parts of the house to pray, about the sixth hour. 10. And, being hungry, he was desirous to taste *somewhat.* And as they

of religion cannot be reconciled with the Gospel of
Jesus Christ. The history of his instruction, baptism,
and reception into the Church occupies so large a
space in the sacred text that it forms the whole of
what is called the tenth chapter of the Acts—a chapter
which consists of forty-eight verses. It looks as if the
Holy Ghost had penned this lengthened description
of this conversion that it might be a standing record
to demolish the flimsy sophistry of those who advocate
unrestricted liberty in the choice of a religious creed.

The good, moral, upright life Cornelius led before
he was baptised by St. Peter, before he had even heard
of St. Peter, corresponds with the picture drawn by
those who hold that it does not matter what creed a
man follows, provided he be a good man after his own

were preparing, there came upon him an ecstasy of mind;
11. And he saw heaven opened, and a certain vessel descending,
as it were a great sheet, let down by the four corners from heaven
to the earth. 12. In which were all manner of four-footed beasts,
and creeping things of the earth, and fowls of the air. 13. And
there came a voice to him: Arise, Peter; kill, and eat. 14. But
Peter said: Far be it from me, Lord; for I have never eaten any
common and unclean thing. 15. And the voice *spoke* to him again
the second time: That which God hath purified, do not thou call
common. 16. And this was done thrice; and presently the vessel
was taken up again into heaven. 17. Now, whilst Peter was
doubting within himself what the vision which he had seen
should mean, behold, the men who were sent by Cornelius,
inquiring for Simon's house, stood at the gate. 18. And when
they had called, they asked if Simon, who is surnamed Peter,
lodged there? 19. And as Peter was thinking on the vision,
the Spirit said to him: Behold, three men seek thee. 20. Arise,
therefore, go down, and go with them, doubting nothing; for
I have sent them. 21. Then Peter, going down to the men,

fashion. *He* surely reaches their standard; for *he* was *truly* a good man after his own fashion, and according to the lights he had received. He was a soldier, but an exceptionally virtuous one. He had a position in the Roman army. He was centurion of the band which was called the Italian band. So far as we can see, he was a man in pretty good circumstances, able to live comfortably. And, as to his moral character, it is described in the second verse of the chapter: " A religious man, and one that feared God with all his house—who gave much alms to the people, and prayed to God always". In the language, then, of inspiration, he is declared to be a good man —to be a man who was full of the fear of God, of the love of God—one who spent long hours in prayer, and

---

said: Behold I am he whom you seek: what is the cause for which you are come ? 22. And they said: Cornelius, a centurion, a just man, and one that feareth God, and that hath good testimony from all the nation of the Jews, received an answer of a holy angel, to send for thee into his house, and to hear words from thee. 23 .Then bringing them in, he lodged them. And the day following he arose, and went with them: and some of the brethren from Joppe accompanied him. 24. And the day after he entered into Cesarea. Now Cornelius was waiting for them, having called together his kinsmen and special friends. 25. And it came to pass when Peter was come in Cornelius met him, and falling down at his feet, worshipped. 26. But Peter raised him up, saying: Rise, I myself also am a man. 27. And talking with him, he went in, and found many that were come together. 28. And he said to them: You know how abominable a thing it is for a man that is a Jew to keep company or to come to one of another nation ; but God hath showed to me not to call any man common or unclean. 29. Wherefore, making no doubt, I came when I was sent for: I ask, therefore,

who divided his substance largely and generously with the poor—one, too, the power of whose example had been such that all the members of his household were influenced by it—walked in uprightness as he did, and practised similar virtues.

Now, what more was wanted? Was he not moving on securely to heaven in his present state? Would he not be sufficiently prepared for a place in heaven by continuing to live as he had lived hitherto? And if the good qualities which are ascribed to him, and the many and exalted virtues he is said to have practised, had been sufficient to qualify him for a place in heaven, why not leave him as he was? Perhaps he was following his present lights better than he would

for what cause you have sent for me? 30. And Cornelius said: Four days ago, until this hour, I was praying in my house at the ninth hour, and, behold, a man stood before me in white apparel, and said: 31. Cornelius, thy prayer is heard, and thy alms are remembered in the sight of God. 32. Send, therefore, to Joppe, and call hither Simon, who is surnamed Peter; he lodgeth in the house of Simon a tanner, by the sea-side. 33. Immediately, therefore, I sent to thee; and thou hast done well in coming. Now, therefore, all we are present in thy sight, to hear all things whatsoever are commanded thee by the Lord. 34. Then Peter, opening his mouth, said: In truth I perceive that God is not a respecter of persons: 35. But in every nation he that feareth Him, and worketh justice, is acceptable to Him. 36. God sent the word to the children of Israel, preaching peace through Jesus Christ (He is Lord of all). 37. You know the word which hath been published through all Judea: for it began from Galilee, after the baptism which John preached. 38. Jesus of Nazareth; how God anointed Him with the Holy Ghost, and with power; who went about doing good, and healing all that were oppressed by the devil; for God was with Him. 39. And we are witnesses of

follow stronger and fuller illuminations, and corresponding with the graces he was actually receiving more
perfectly than he would correspond with more abundant ones. Why, then, not leave him as he was?—why
take any further trouble with him? God, however,
did not leave him as he was; *He* condescended to
take further trouble with him, if I may be allowed that
familiar way of expressing the idea. He sent an
angel from heaven to Cornelius. And the angel, in
the name of Him who sent him, commanded Cornelius to invite St. Peter, that St. Peter might come
and instruct him and the members of his family as to
what they must do. The angel was not content with
giving a vague general command. He did not leave

all things which He did in the land of the Jews and in Jerusalem;
whom they killed, hanging Him upon a tree. 40. Him God
raised up the third day, and gave Him to be made manifest.
41. Not to all the people, but to witnesses preordained of God,
even to us, who ate and drank with Him after He rose again from
the dead. 42. And He commanded us to preach to the people,
and to testify that it is He who hath been appointed by God to
be the judge of the living and of the dead. 43. To Him all the
prophets give testimony, that through His name all receive remis-
sion of sins who believe in Him. 44. While Peter was yet speaking these words, the Holy Ghost fell upon all them that were
hearing the word. 45. And the faithful of the circumcision, who
had come with Peter, were astonished because the grace of the
Holy Ghost was also poured out upon the Gentiles. 46. For
they heard them speaking with tongues and magnifying God.
47. Then Peter answered: Can any man forbid water, that these
should not be baptised, who have received the Holy Ghost as
well as we? 48. And he commanded them to be baptised in
the name of the Lord Jesus Christ. Then they entreated him to
stay with them some days,

Cornelius in doubt as to where St. Peter was to be found. He told him that Peter was in the city of Joppe, described the quarter of the city in which he abode, and mentioned the very house in which he was staying. Cornelius promptly and gladly obeyed this message from heaven. He at once sent three men to Joppe to invite him to his house in Cesarea. As these three men were approaching Joppe, St. Peter himself had a vision. At the end of this vision, the Spirit of God said to him that three men stood at the door seeking him—that they had been divinely sent, and that he was to go with them whither they would lead him. The following day he set out for Cesarea, accompanied by the messengers who had come to invite him. And the morrow after he reached the house of the centurion, instructed him and the members of his household in the true Gospel, and received them into the one true Church.

Now, here the advocates of Indifferentism are on the horns of a dilemma. *One* of two conclusions they are forced to draw—namely, either God sends His Apostles, and *even* His angels, on useless errands, or it cannot be a matter of indifference to Him what religion people profess. If Cornelius knew God, if he feared Him, if he loved Him—if he loved Him, too, in His poor by relieving those who were in distress—if he spent long hours in prayer, if his life was such that he was styled in inspired language a "just man," why should God send an angel from heaven to him, or why should He send St. Peter from Joppe to Cesarea, to bring to him the light of the new

Gospel, to administer to him the sacrament of baptism, and to receive him and his family into the one true fold?

On the other hand, when St. Peter, as an Apostle of the new religion, stood in the presence of Cornelius, and put before him the doctrines of that religion, was he (Cornelius) free to keep any longer to the old form of worship in which he had served God for some time before, and to reject the doctrines which Peter had come expressly to announce to him? Or, was he free to accept some of those doctrines and to reject others? If he had hesitated, or if he had made it a condition of his being received into the Church, that he could go back to his own old religion after a time, in case he preferred to do so when he had given the new one a fair trial, and that he was to have the free exercise of his private judgment as to the meaning he was to attach to the Gospel truths, would St. Peter have admitted him into the fold of Christ? Certainly not. And above all, if after a visit from an angel of heaven —if while there stood in his presence an Apostle who had been divinely instructed in a vision to come to him—if while it was clear as noonday it was God's will he should abandon his old religion and take to the new—if in spite of all this he had persisted in still clinging to the old one, saying that it was the one he had been most used to, at least for some time—that he did not ask for a better, that he did not care for novelties and changes, that he dreaded the wrench which such a change must bring with it, that he shrank from breaking with relations and friends, that he feared to incur their dislike, that he might lose his position in the Roman army, that such a step might reduce himself and his family to penury, and that in consequence of these many grave and well-founded fears, he had made up his mind to remain as he was—that he would keep in the old lines, pray as much as he had prayed before, give alms more abundantly still, and do good to all within his reach. Now, had he reasoned thus and acted thus, and remained in his old religion, while heaven's light flashed upon him with such overwhelming brightness, that he saw as clearly as he saw the sun in the heavens that it was wrong to remain in it any longer, would that old religion, and his many virtues, and his many prayers, and his abundant alms have availed him aught for heaven? No; God had now revealed to him the creed which He commanded him to embrace, and he (Cornelius) was not free to put it aside and to follow some other creed instead. He might pray, he might profess to live in the fear of God, he might give all his substance to feed the poor—all would be in vain, unless he gave up his old form of worship, which for *him* could no longer be right, and adhere to that new faith which God, through His Angel and His Apostle, had shown him to be the true one, and the only true one. "Without faith it is impossible to please God" (*Heb.* xi. 6).

The application of this to current events is already implied, in the supposition I have made with regard to Cornelius, in the event of his having failed or neglected to take the course which he had the happiness to follow.

Before entering upon this application, I feel I ought to ask the reader's indulgence while I digress for a short time from the main line of argument. I have less hesitation in asking this permission, as the application itself, though it is a slight departure from the direct line of demonstration, embodies, nevertheless, a further refutation of the pernicious system against which I am arguing.

A man, belonging to some non-Catholic denomination, seeing the number of rich, respectable, educated people who leave the ranks of Protestantism and enter the Catholic Church, may become unhinged in the creed he has hitherto professed. He begins to have doubts, and serious ones, as to whether that creed is right or wrong. In spite of the prejudices generated by early education, in spite of those popular calumnies which taught him in his boyhood and early youth that any religion was better than the Roman one— that all Churches were good enough, *except* the Roman Church, he has, nevertheless, a sort of incipient, though reluctant, leaning towards the faith which that Church teaches. Natural motives incline him to remain where he is; something abnormal within him (which he cannot explain to himself) impels him in another direction. He stands bewildered in the clash of so many contending, antagonistic creeds; his reason tells him that all cannot be right, that one only can be right, and he is quite uncertain whether he belongs to the one which is right, or to one amongst the many which are wrong. He doubts more seriously every day.

Well, such a man either seeks to have his doubts

cleared up or he does not. If he is sincerely anxious to find a solution of them, he will set the right way about it—*i.e.*, he will put himself to the trouble of inquiring, of reading, of consulting; he will pray with earnestness, and with his whole heart, for light from on high; and if he continue to pray earnestly and heartily for light, light is sure to come. The darkness of error and the mists of doubt will gradually disappear. No angel may be sent to him from heaven, and no Apostle of the true faith may be divinely instructed on earth to come to him; but the light of reason and the light of revelation combined may show him—and show him so clearly that he can no longer have any rational doubt about the matter—that his present religion is wrong, and that the one he was taught in his younger years to ridicule and to hold in detestation is the right one, and the *only* right one.

The course he is bound to follow under these circumstances is evident. He is bound to take, energetically and promptly, the final step which will lead him into that Church to which the steady light of faith is inviting him. The same grace which is a star to guide him is meant to be also a help to direct his steps in the path it traces out for him. Not to correspond with that grace, which is at once both light and strength, is to abuse it, and to abuse it is to run the risk of losing it for ever; for no man has control over the length of time he is to live, or the measure of grace he is to have; and the worst way to get grace in the future is to throw away the grace which is given in the present. I say he is bound to follow, promptly and energetically, the light which is made to shine upon him, and to use the strength which is divinely given him ; for God does not give His supernatural helps in vain. When *He* communicates His lights and His strength, He expects, and He has a right to expect, that they will be used for the purpose for which they are bestowed ; and He will demand at the judgment-seat a rigorous account from those who, through apathy, cowardice, or caprice, shut their eyes to His light, or waste those helps which are meant to strengthen them on the way to the true fold.

Such a man may pray a great deal, may perform acts of heroic penance ; he may speak with the tongues of men and of angels, he may distribute all his goods to feed the poor, his portrait may hang in every drawing-room, his bust or statue may be found in every place of public resort, he may wield a wide influence amongst his fellow-men, he may have the good testimony of all who know him, he may be a useful, benevolent, beneficent member of society, he may be the very ideal of a philanthropist, he may impress all who come in contact with him that he is a good man after his own fashion—all this will fail to save him, if he refuses or neglects to enter that Church which he sees in the irresistible light of faith to be the true one, and the only true one. Without faith it is impossible to please God. Which that Church is to which his star must guide him, if faithfully followed, we shall determine later on, in the second part of this little book, when we discuss the external marks which must necessarily belong to the true Church, and which can belong to her alone.

This leads us to the further treatment of the second part of our supposition—*i.e.*, to consider in detail the position of the man who does not seek a solution of his doubts, and who strives to drown the voice of conscience by endeavouring to argue himself into the conviction that good works with any form of Christian belief are a sufficient qualification for the kingdom of heaven.

In spite of his efforts to stifle the voice of conviction, his doubts become more grave every day; for he cannot help noticing the stream of conversions which is constantly flowing into the Catholic Church. He observes that every year several men of standing, of great ability, of varied learning, leave the Protestant and embrace the Catholic communion. He understands perfectly well that they cannot be doing so from motives of self-interest. He has penetration enough to perceive that in taking such a step they have nothing to gain in a temporal point of view, but everything to lose. He has heard repeatedly that many of them made the change with the certain knowledge that they would lose in consequence their family inheritance, a rich living, an annual income, a lucrative business, a good situation, a means of livelihood—that they would be disowned and cast off by their nearest and dearest relatives, have to break some of the fondest family ties, incur the displeasure of many cherished friends, and lose the respect of large numbers of old and highly-esteemed acquaintance.

He looks at some of the late prominent dignitaries of the Catholic Church in England, and he finds that the history of what they were in the not very distant past is still fresh in the memories of all. That contemporary history tells him that some of the greatest intellects that England has ever produced, that some of the brightest stars that ever shone in the English Protestant Church, in this century abandoned her, and gave their life, genius, heart, soul, whole being, to another Church. That same history makes it clear to him that these great men did not give up Protestantism without counting the cost. Numberless difficulties stared them in the face—difficulties which would have appalled and unnerved men of less force of will, or would at least have made them try to find principles of expediency to baffle conviction. And souls less brave and hearts less courageous might have succumbed before getting even half-way over the dark waters that separate Protestantism from Catholicity. They had England at their feet while they remained members of the Establishment; on the other hand, they felt as if they themselves must ever sit at the feet of the humblest members of the priesthood of the communion they were embracing. The high places, to which the Catholic Church was in time to lift them, were still far below the horizon, could hardly be dreamt of (at least by themselves) as things within the range of possibility. They could not foresee the glories which were to crown their courage, and make them shine as beacons in the Church of their adoption. The panorama they had to contemplate was, in an earthly point of view, dark beyond description. The loss, not merely for a time, but for ever, of the high place they had hitherto occupied—the loss of revenues, the loss, too, of the prestige with which fame had already invested their name as champions of the faith they had till then professed, the sacrifice of prospects which made the highest elevations in the Protestant hierarchy far more than probable; on the other hand, nothing to look forward to in the Church to which they were submitting but a position of insignificance, crosses, humiliations, perpetual self-denial, and a life of comparative obscurity—such the contrast between the fascinations of the delightful life they were renouncing, and the stern rigours of the life of abnegation for which they girded themselves up, when they resolved to take the course in which unchanging conviction was irresistibly drawing them. They had all the merit of that heroic, unlimited self-sacrifice which their will cheerfully embraced when they took the step which severed them for ever from the Church of their family, and which lodged them safely in the bosom of the old Church of Rome.

Our friend (who doubts) philosophises on the conversion of men such as I have been describing. He feels that nothing but the force of conviction, deep and irresistible, could have led them on in this course, could have made them brave such dangers and nerve them for such sacrifices. It occurs to him, too, that if men of such undoubted uprightness, such ability, such learning—men who were so conversant with the question of religion, who were thoroughly qualified to compare the relative merits of different creeds, made up their minds in the face of such formidable obstacles to abjure the Church in which they had been brought up, and to make their submission to another—then other men of less ability, of less knowledge, and of fewer opportunities of judging, and who were brought up in the same Church, ought at least to doubt.

It may have been in reasoning of this kind that his own first doubts had their origin. And since the day when he first became unsettled in the creed of his family, the news of each successive notable conversion has tended to render his doubts more disquieting and more perplexing. He feels impelled to draw the conclusion that those great, able, learned, religious-minded men, who had so many motives to bind them to the Church of their birth and early years, would never have renounced her at the cost of such sacrifices, if they had entertained the idea that they could have saved their souls equally easily, or saved them *at all*, in the religion taught by the Church which they were abandoning. This process of reasoning may lead him still further, and may incline him to draw the additional inference, namely, that if other members of the Establishment, who have remained listless in their doubts for years, had applied their mind to the search after the true faith, with that energy and indomitable perseverance with which they give themselves up to temporal pursuits, there would have been a far greater number who would have followed in the path traced out by those heroic souls who have so nobly and so courageously sacrificed everything in their glorious search after the truth.

Such his doubts, such the facts that have generated them, such the reflections that have increased them. Still in *his* case they lead to no practical result. And it is his own fault that they do not. He can reason cleverly enough about the conversion of others, and speak eloquently about the conclusions which such conversions ought to incline people to draw. But, though he is full of uncertainties and perplexities himself, he takes no means to have them cleared up. He is tossed about on the ocean of error, and he makes no effort whatever to get on the dry and firm land. Nor can it be argued, in extenuation of this culpable apathy, that he is ignorant of the dangers which surround his present position. He has no difficulty in realising the gravity, the vital importance, of the point at issue. He knows that religion has to do with the soul, and that the soul is immortal—that with regard to himself it is a question of eternal life or eternal death ; and that in reference to God it is a question of serving Him according to the form of worship He has prescribed, or some other form of worship at variance with the one on which He has set the seal of Divine sanction.

All this he fully understands ; and he fully understands, moreover, the terrible consequences which must attend his want of decision. Though harassed by so many disquietudes and perplexities about matters of religion, he nevertheless enjoys a sort of lethargic peace of soul. While his conscience is oppressed by a multitude of doubts, he chooses practically to ignore them. And if his state of mind is analysed, it may be described in this form, namely: " I have serious doubts as to the truth of the religion which I nominally profess. I have various reasons for thinking it is not the religion of Christ. I feel unaccountably and irresistibly drawn to another which I have been taught hitherto to despise and to hate. I am quite uncertain whether I am serving God in the right way or the wrong way ; and although I am pretty sure I could find out for certain which is the religion in which He wishes me to serve Him if I made the effort, still I will give myself no trouble about it. I know that I ought to inquire, but inquiry is irksome and inconvenient, and if once begun and followed up it may show me the necessity of making changes from the very thought of which I shrink with horror. Many good men, who are as much bound to inquire as I am, hold that it is a matter of no consequence what form of Christian belief a man professes, provided he be a man of good works. I will remain as I am. I will keep to the creed I was brought up in. I will do as much in the way of good works as I can. I will lead as good a life as possible. And, as to matters of faith, I will take my chance." This may not be recognised as expressing the state of mind of a certain class of Indifferentists, but I think it will be generally admitted that it expresses the state of mind of many.

Now here we are engaged in a hand-to-hand combat with our opponents. The defenders of the system of Indifferentism, if true to their principles, will hold that this man is quite secure as far as religion is concerned, that he is a good man after his own fashion, and that he has nothing whatever to fear in regard to the world to come.

I maintain that such a man cannot possibly be a good man in *God's* sense of the word "good" so long as he remains wilfully and apathetically in the state of doubt in which he is living at present. He lacks the very foundation of supernatural goodness—*i.e.*, that firm, unswerving faith, without which no superstructure of supernatural virtue can be raised. His faith, shifting like the sands of the beach, is equivalent to no faith at all. It means everything and it means nothing; for it means nothing *definite*. In the secret of his heart he sets more value on a creed to which he is supposed to be antagonistic than he does on the one which he nominally professes. And yet he has not the courage or strength of will to enter upon a search after the solution of his doubts. Self-interest, human respect, craven fear, downright apathy, sheer indifference, prevent him from doing so. The things of time absorb nearly all his attention; he has none to give to the settlement of the question on which his eternal state depends. While he willingly takes an immense deal of trouble in arranging the affairs of his house, of his family, of his business, in seeking after the situation, occupation, or work which brings the largest wage, in attending to an infinity of trifles, he takes no trouble at all (although he is harassed by constant misgivings about the matter) in assuring himself whether he is doing rightly or wrongly that

greatest and most important of all duties—the duty he
was sent into the world to do—the duty of serving
God. "Fear God, and keep His commandments; for
this is all man" (*Ecclesiastes* xii. 13). Can we say that
the man who attaches so little importance to God's
service, that he does not care whether he is serving
Him in the way that He approves of, or in a way
that He condemns, is practising in any degree that
holy fear spoken of in the inspired language which I
have quoted?

Does not the first precept of the Decalogue forbid
not only the worship of strange gods, but also the
worship of the *true God* in a way that is false and
wrong? On what foundation then can that man rest
the confident hope of being eternally saved who has
good reason to believe that he is not worshipping his
Creator according to the fashion He has divinely
revealed, but according to a bundle of erroneous
doctrines and empty rites which have had their origin
in the pride and obstinate opinionativeness of novelty-
seeking men? Is God likely to give heaven to those
who will not condescend to inquire which is the road
that leads to it? No. Heaven is the greatest reward
which in His omnipotence He can bestow. He will
never give it to the man who doubts seriously whether
he is walking in the way that leads towards it or the
way that leads *away from* it, and who does not think
it worth his while to make inquiries, though he has
easy and ample opportunities of doing so. If it still
be urged that he is a good man after his own fashion,
I answer, that may be; but he is not a good man after

God's fashion, and on that everything depends. That moral goodness which God demands as a qualification for heaven can never be found in the soul which is oscillating (entirely through its own fault) in vague, perpetual uncertainty, or which is deliberately stifling doubts, instead of continuing to inquire with a view to finding a solution of them.

Hence, I hold that the very terms in which the theory of Indifferentism is enunciated are sophistical —at least, if it is a question of a man into whose mind has come a reasonable suspicion that he is wrong. For that system supposes something *as proved* which is *not* proved, which never *can* be proved, for the simple reason that such a thing is an impossibility. It supposes that a man *can* be a good man, *even* according to the Divine standard of goodness, although he is in constant wilful doubt whether he is offering to God a worship which is agreeable to Him, or a worship which He must disown and reject. And *can* that great God, who is just and holy and true, ever look upon as good the man who lives day by day in grave doubt, in sheer indifference, whether he is glorifying Him by believing what is true, or insulting Him by professing a creed which he has good reason to believe may be false? God is the God of truth. He must love truth of necessity; and by the same law of His Divine being, He must bear an everlasting and unchanging hatred to what is contrary thereto.

The striking words of the Cardinal Archbishop of Westminster in reference to this are in place here. Alluding to a kindred subject (*i.e.*, " Rationalism the legitimate consequence of private judgment"), he says: "Greater things than argument are at stake— the honour of our Lord and the eternal salvation of souls. How great is the dishonour, of which men think so little; as if truth were a sort of coin, that they may stamp and change, and vary its die and fix its value, and make it in metal or paper as they will! They treat the truth as one of the elements of human barter, or as an indulgence which a man may hold and use for himself alone, leaving his neighbour to perish. This is truth to me; look you to what you believe. What dishonour is this to the person of our Lord? Picture to yourselves this night upon your knees the throne of the Son of God; cherubim and seraphim adoring the glory of Eternal Truth, the changeless light of the Incarnate Word, yesterday, to-day, and for ever the same; the heavenly court replenished with the illumination of God, the glorified intelligences, in whose pure spirit the thought of falsehood is hateful as the thought of sin;—then look to earth on those whom the blood of Christ hath redeemed; look on those who in this world should have inherited the faith; look at their controversies, their disputes, their doubts, their misery; and in the midst of all these wandering, sinning, perishing souls, look at those who stand by in selfish, cold complacency, wrapping themselves in their own opinion, and saying, 'This is truth to me'. Think, too, of the souls that perish. How many are brought into the very gulf of eternal death through uncertainty? How, as every pastor can tell you, souls are torn from the hand which would save them by being sedulously taught that the deadliest sins have no sin in them; by the specious and poisonous insinuation that sin has no moral quality; how souls have first been sapped in their faith as Satan began in Paradise. 'Yea, hath God said?' that is, God hath not said. This is perpetually at this hour going on around us: and whence comes it? Because men have cast down the Divine authority, and have substituted in its place the authority of men, that is, of each man for himself" (*Grounds of Faith*, pp. 84, 85).

I now return to the argument drawn from the conversion of the centurion: and I return to it to answer an objection.

I am well aware that the patrons of Indifferentism will appeal to a certain portion of the chapter (*Acts* x.) as containing a vindication of their theory. They quote the thirty-fourth and thirty-fifth verses as a clear and explicit defence of it. In these verses we find St. Peter, after hearing from the lips of Cornelius an account of the wonderful way in which he had been visited by an angel, and commanded to send for him, giving expression to his thankful admiration of God's loving providence in leading pure-minded men into the true Church. These verses run thus: "And Peter opening his mouth said: In very deed I perceive that God is not a respecter of persons. But in every nation, he that feareth Him and worketh justice, is acceptable to Him" (*Acts* x. 34, 35).

Now, the supporters of Indifferentism, looking at these words quite apart from the context and from the exceptional circumstances in which they were spoken, seem to think that they warrant almost any conclusion ; and they have no scruple in drawing a very wide one. They say (at least some of them say) that it is evident, from this emphatic declaration of the Apostle, that God does not care what a man is, in point of religion —that He is quite indifferent whether he is a Jew or a Gentile, a Pagan, or a Turk, a Presbyterian, a Protestant, a Ritualist, or even a Roman Catholic (if you will), provided he be an honest, straightforward, benevolent, charitable man.

Let us see if there is anything in the verses in question to justify this bold reasoning. Can these words of St. Peter be construed, even by the most subtle understanding of them, into a vindication of the theory of Indifferentism ? No, certainly not. For, quite apart from their true meaning, as made evident by the context, the very circumstances even, in which they were spoken, embody an unanswerable refutation of any such theory. If God were indifferent as to what form of worship His creatures paid Him, then St. Peter's visit on that occasion to Cornelius was useless—his long journey of more than a day from Joppe to Cesarea was useless—the journey of the three men who travelled so far to invite him was useless—the coming of the angel from heaven was useless—the truths Peter announced to him were useless, and would have served the purpose quite as well if they had been but a repetition of the old doctrines of the Synagogue, or a rehearsal of those fragments of revelation which were already familiar to Cornelius —the baptism was useless, an idle ceremony which might have been very conveniently replaced by some of the old rites of the Jewish ceremonial. In such a supposition these long journeys and the consequent fatigue, the preparatory instructions given to the centurion and his family before reception into the Church, the performance of the sacred functions by which they were made members of the Church—all this might have been dispensed with; and so all parties might have been spared a great deal of unnecessary trouble. But can we conceive a God of infinite wisdom, who must have an end in everything He does, going beyond the lines of His ordinary providence, working great miracles, employing so many intermediate agents—*i.e.*, servants, Apostles, angels— to lead a man who was already acceptable to Him to a knowledge of a certain definite creed, if He cared so little about matters of faith as the advocates of Indifferentism would have us believe? Is not the secret why these propagandists of broad Christianity give to the passage in question so free and wide an interpretation patent to every reasonable man who thoughtfully investigates the matter? Is it not this? They would have it that God must be indifferent about religion, just because *they* are disposed to be indifferent about it themselves. They paint Him, not according to the dictates of intimate conviction, but according to the bent of natural inclination; and they cling to Indifferentism as a creed, not because they believe it is one which is particularly calculated to give Him glory, but because it is one that is particularly suited to their own convenience. It presupposes little restraint; still, quite as much as they are disposed to bear. It is an excuse for a religion, while it leaves them free to believe what they like, and, with regard to many points, perhaps to do what they like. In point of convenience, there is nothing that has the resemblance of a Christian creed that can be compared with it. It saves people from the reproach of being absolute unbelievers, while it gives them unlimited latitude both as to articles of faith and as to the laws of moral conduct. In fact it may be said to be diluted idolatry; for those who profess it make God not what He is, but what they wish Him to be—that is, as careless and indifferent about His religion as the most careless and indifferent amongst His creatures.

But now having considered the circumstances in which the words were spoken, let us sift the meaning of the words themselves. "In very deed," said St. Peter, "I perceive that God is not a respecter of persons. But in every nation he that feareth Him and worketh justice is acceptable to Him." The real meaning is evidently this. 1st. That God does not exclude the Gentiles from the gifts of faith and of grace, and that He is as willing to receive Gentiles as Jews into His Church. 2nd. That while He is free to give or to withhold from men the gifts of His grace, which are quite gratuitous, He at the same time has no regard to a man's race, or lineage, or pedigree, or country, or nationality, when there is question of the distribution of those gifts; in other words, that the being a member of a particular race, or a native of a particular country, is not demanded by Him as a pre-requisite for becoming acceptable to Him, or for finding favour in His eyes. 3rd. That if a man knows God and fears Him, and leads a just life accord-ing to the supernatural lights which are given him, and does the works of justice with the aid of Divine grace, according to his present knowledge of religion, while he is yet in invincible ignorance that there is any other religion which is true, or, at all events, that there is any other which is better than his own, and if he is in such a frame of mind that in case it were made evident to him that his old religion can be no longer right for *him*, he would be quite willing to abandon it, and quite willing, on the other hand, to embrace another as soon as he became absolutely certain it was the Divine Will he should do so—then such a man, whether he was born in Judea or Galilee, or in some heathen land, like Job, shall find favour with God.

This *must* be the meaning of Peter's words, for it is evident Cornelius himself is the ideal Peter is describ-ing. He (Peter) is contemplating a man whose cir-cumstances in regard to religion, whose tone of mind, and whose dispositions of heart resembled those of the centurion. And hence the widest conclusion that must be drawn from his words is, that God looks with favour on those who live in holy fear and lead a just life according to their lights, as Cornelius did, and who, having no knowledge of a better way of serving Him at present, are ready to adopt a new and a higher form of worship as soon as it is His good pleasure to reveal it to them. It is to people who act up to their lights in this way St. Thomas alludes when he teaches that it is to be held as *most certain* that God will either, by some interior inspiration, reveal to them what is of necessary belief for salvation, or will send them some preacher of the faith, as He sent St. Peter to Cornelius, rather than let them perish through want of faith. His words are: "Si enim aliquis, taliter nutritus, ductum naturalis rationis sequeretur in appetitu boni et fugâ mali, certissime est tenendum quod ei Deus vel per internam inspirationem revelaret ea quæ sunt ad credendum necessaria vel aliquem fidei prædicatorem ad eum dirigeret, sicut misit Petrum ad Cornelium" (*De fide*, 2-14, Art. xi.). He is treating the case of a man who lives in a place where none of the ordinary or natural means of attaining to a knowledge of Divine revelation are to be found. The conversion of Cornelius is, indeed, a striking illustration of the truth of the teaching of this great doctor of the Church.

But the meaning of the verses in question will become still more clear if we look at the matter from another point of view. Suppose that St. Peter, as soon as he reached Cesarea, perceived that Cornelius, in the short interval between the vision of the angel and his own arrival at his house, had changed his mind again, and had begun to resist God's will though it had been so clearly manifested to him ; and suppose that he declared to Peter that although he knew with absolute certainty the religion he came to announce to him was now the only true one—that it was the

Divine Will he should embrace it at *once*, and that it was wrong for him to follow the old one any longer—still, having regard to the tremendous temporal difficulties which, for a man in his position, stood in the way, he could not think of making the sacrifices which such a step demanded, would St. Peter, in such a supposition, have spoken words which implied that he (Cornelius) was there and then acceptable to God? Every reasonable man must answer, No; for although Cornelius had been (or in case he had been) in the Divine favour till then—till the hour came when there was question of corresponding with or rejecting the signal grace then offered, he would have sinned the moment he wilfully and persistently rejected it. And his sin would have been the particularly great sin of the man who, while heaven's light was shining upon him with its brightest rays to show him what was false on one side and what was true on the other, chose falsehood in preference to truth, and did so from motives of self-interest, and in open resistance to God's will.

Till the apparition of the angel, or a little before, Cornelius, though knowing the one true God, and having implicit faith in Christ the Mediator, had been living in invincible ignorance that there was a higher and a holier religion than that which he was practising; but that ignorance had begun now to be vincible. The announcement that the promulgation of the Gospel of Christ had been made at Jerusalem on the day of Pentecost was spreading widely. It had already reached several cities of the Roman provinces, and

Cornelius had probably heard tidings of it from the Jews with whom he associated at Cesarea. At all events, that Gospel had now been promulgated to himself, personally, in a manner so wonderful and so miraculous that there was no longer room for any doubt. Had he turned a deaf ear to the truths it announced and the laws it imposed, he would have sinned, and lost by his sin the grace he had hitherto possessed, or the favour of God, in whose eyes he had till then been acceptable.

Our opponents are not disconcerted. They hold that the conversion of Cornelius, and the arguments we have drawn from it, do not weaken their position in the least. Although Cornelius knew the true God, they observe, still he had not explicit faith in Christ the Mediator; nor had he been as yet instructed in the fundamental doctrines of Christianity. But *we*, they urge, are Christians, and *as* such we believe those great and broad truths on which Christianity is built. We hold, however, that within the limits of those broad and wide fundamental truths, it is lawful to construct several different creeds, and creeds, too, which on many points contradict each other.

This reasoning is easily answered. It carries with it its own refutation. That the sophistry it contains may be more thoroughly exposed and our answer to it appear in clearer light, we must look again at some of the doctrines on which the principal Christian creeds differ, and at the same time keep before our minds the momentous importance of those doctrines. These creeds differ on the doctrine of the Real

Presence of Christ in the Eucharist, on the doctrine of sacramental confession, on the question of the Pope's jurisdiction. They also differ as to whether there is a voice on earth which is infallible when it speaks on certain matters in certain given circumstances. Now, surely it is a matter of importance whether Christ is or is not truly and really present in the Sacrament of the Eucharist, whether confession is or is not the ordinary means instituted by Christ for obtaining forgiveness of the grievous sins committed after baptism, whether the Supreme Pontiff has or has *not* universal spiritual jurisdiction over the whole world, and whether he is or is *not* infallible when he speaks in his character of universal teacher on matters of faith and morals. Could there be doctrines which affect the interests of men's souls more deeply than these? With this question we proceed to answer the statement of the Indifferentist: that within the limits of the broad and wide fundamental truths on which Christianity is built it is lawful to construct different creeds, and creeds even which on many points contradict each other.

What is Christianity? We do not ask for an elaborate definition drawn from any theological treatise. Better not use such, perhaps, as the authority of the theological school from which it issued might be questioned. We shall take the usual or common definition or description found in almost every dictionary, which is to this effect: Christianity is the religion taught by Christ.

Now, the religion taught by Christ was one in its

beginning, it has been one ever since, and it must ever remain one to the end of time. It cannot be two. It cannot differ from itself; if it could, it would not be Christ's. As there is only one true Baptism, says St. Paul, one true Saviour, one true God and Father of all, so there can be only one true faith. "Careful to keep the unity of the Spirit in the bond of peace. One body and one spirit, as you are called in one hope of your calling; one Lord, one faith, one Baptism, one God and Father of all, who is above all, and through all, and in us all" (*Ephes.* iv. 3-6). In other words, Christianity, as it signifies the religion revealed by Christ, means truth. For Christ is the God of truth, who cannot speak a lie. And truth is one—it is something pure and simple. It is not a compound consisting of various elements, some of which are true and others false. It can admit no alloy of falsehood without losing its essence, without ceasing to be what it is. Light and darkness cannot co-exist; heat and cold cannot be found in the same place at the same time. Falsehood and truth cannot be built together on Christ, who, as the God of truth, is the foundation on which His religion rests. To affirm, then, that, within the broad and wide limits of Christianity, different creeds, and even contradictory creeds, may be lawfully built up, is simply to affirm that Christ's religion may mean truth and falsehood at once—may be a mixture of what is true and what is false; and that Christ Himself meant it to be such, since, if He did not mean it to be such, it would be against all reason to hold that contradictory creeds

6

may lawfully spring out of it. But was not that religion true in all its parts when Christ delivered it to His Apostles, to be propagated throughout the world? And was it not true in all its parts when His Apostles transmitted it to their successors? And was it not that it might remain true in all its parts, free from all alloy of falsehood to the end of time, that He promised to send His Spirit, the Spirit of truth, to teach all truth; and promised, too, to be with His Church Himself all days even to the consummation of the world?

Could He mean, when He revealed those doctrines which were to constitute Christianity, that He left men free to give them contradictory forms according as fancy or inclination prompted? Had even the Apostles themselves any power to change them, or to leave people free to believe their opposites, as they thought fit? And if the Apostles, to whose guardianship they were committed, could not change them in the least item, how does it appear that any innovator or new evangelist, who has come into the world since their day, has had any authority to take such liberty with them? What passage is there in the whole range of Scripture from Genesis to the Apocalypse—what has there been handed down in tradition—what is there in the dictates of right reason to justify the assumption that Christ meant to leave people free to draw contradictory creeds out of the religion which He revealed? Does not everything in Scripture, in tradition, in reason, point the other way? I have never heard, you, dear reader, have never heard, no one has ever heard, that He said at any time, that if men believed the unity of God, the Trinity, the Incarnation, and the Redemption, they might be free about all the other dogmas of His revelation.

But, quite independently of reasoning of this kind, the statement is refuted from the very words in which it is made. It leads to conclusions the most absurd. To say that, within the limits of the great fundamental doctrines of Christianity, there is room for different creeds, and creeds which on many points contradict each other, is hardly anything less than a contradiction in terms. For if such liberty is allowed, Christianity can never have any limits at all. In other words, while the theory of Indifferentism may be said to have certain limits to begin with, it has none whatever to end with. It can be expanded to any degree its upholder wishes, be stretched out indefinitely, and be made to mean anything and everything, or nothing, according to men's whims, fancies, caprices, private judgment, most foolish eccentricities. There is no restrictive or restraining element in it to check its course. It is necessarily progressive, changeful, variable. Freedom of opinion is its principle of life; and freedom of opinion has never recognised any limits in the past, nor is there any hope it will ever recognise any in the future. The only sphere in which it finds itself at home is illimitable space. There is no anchor to keep it within fixed distance. It is like a puny boat, unfastened from its moorings, swept over the ocean by the rage of the tempest, without steersman, without rudder, without chart, at the mercy of every wind and wave.

Here is the secret why the religion of the Reformation has been divided, and subdivided, and re-sub-divided into numberless sects. It claimed the right of liberty of opinion, of individual preference; it repudiated the idea of being bound to obey any controlling or authoritative voice that could keep it within definite lines. Hence, its doctrines, like circles on the water, became wider and wider as time went on. These doctrines are expanding still every day; and it is not unreasonable to say that the only thing that will put an end to their constant expansion will be the day of general judgment.

But perhaps we shall be told that even in the Church of Rome, which boasts to be so clear and definite in her teachings, liberty of opinion with regard to certain matters of doctrine is allowed, and that in all such matters members of her communion may hold different and even contradictory views. Why, then, condemn in another Church what we approve in our own? Is it not unfair to deny to others a right which we, to a certain extent, make use of ourselves? What is the difference, ask our opponents, between our system and that followed by the Church of Rome? Is it not this, that while *she* marks off the limits of liberty of opinion at a certain point, we make those limits a little wider? She gives a certain amount of latitude, we give a little more. The difference, therefore, is a difference, *not* of kind, but of degree.

We shall not seek to evade the difficulty. We shall meet it fairly, face to face. And we say at once it is not a difference of degree, but an essential difference of principle between the Catholic and non-Catholic Churches. Catholics recognise the infallible voice of the Church as the divinely established means of securing unity in faith, by fixing the limits of free thought and necessary faith. But non-Catholics sanction the right of private judgment, which is a principle not of unity, but of division and diversity. We readily admit that there are certain things in which the Catholic Church allows her children liberty of opinion. But the very lines within which she circumscribes that liberty may be regarded as an additional, though an implicit, proof of her truthfulness. She marks out clearly the limits up to which liberty may go, beyond which it must *never* go. "Thus far," she says to her children, "you may go in the exercise of freedom of opinion, but no farther."

She defines, too, with equal clearness, the sphere within which necessary faith is demanded, and demanded under penalties of the gravest kind. And so authoritative is her voice, and so distinctly does she draw the lines that mark the boundaries both of liberty and of obligation, that if one of her own children persistently held that there was no liberty of belief where she granted it, she would cease to regard him as a member of her communion, and would brand him at once with the mark of heresy. Nor would she be less stern in pronouncing upon him the sentence of excommunication if he obstinately refused to submit his understanding to any of those great and distinctly revealed truths which she binds her members, under pain of heresy, to believe. More than this; if, in order to meet some dangerous innovation, she brings a certain doctrine into more striking prominence, and clothes it in a new garb, though an old truth, so as to meet the heresy it is meant to combat and to crush, any of her members persistently refuses to subscribe to her definition, she condemns him at once in the most emphatic terms, and cuts him off unhesitatingly from her communion.

Surely there is a great difference between a religion which is secured by bulwarks such as these against the assaults of Rationalism, and a religion which, I may say, consists of nothing else but Rationalism, which is made up of those favourite doctrines which free inquiry, guided by tastes and inclinations, leads a man to choose as his formula of belief. Wide, indeed, is the distance that separates the man who belongs to a Church which, under penalties such as I have named, demands submission to her teachings, from the man who makes his own fancy and caprice the only measure of his faith and the only standard of his morality.

The Church of Christ makes religion something clear, distinct, definite; Indifferentism makes it something so vague and so variable, that it reduces it to nothing. That Church, pointing to her teachings, says to her children : " These are the doctrines which I, in Christ's name, declare have been divinely revealed. These you are bound to believe. In whatever else there may be liberty of opinion, there can be no liberty here."

The system of Indifferentism, on the contrary, authorises its disciples to look through the whole series of Christian creeds, just as they would look through the range of stalls at a bazaar; gives them full freedom to patronise the one which most commends itself to their taste—with the additional privilege of giving it up when they get tired of it, and of patronising some other in preference when fancy, family connection, matrimonial alliance, self-interest, greater convenience, or anything else whatever inclines them to do so.

The Church of Christ makes religion consist in God's unchanging revelation; Indifferentism makes it consist in man's ever-changing opinion. The Church of Christ insists on belief in one definite creed; Indifferentism openly and boldly sanctions the lawfulness of holding as many antagonistic creeds as there are men who hold antagonistic opinions. Which system has the stronger claim to be judged true?

CHAPTER IV.

Refutation of Indifferentism from the History of the Council of Jerusalem.

THE Apostles realised fully that they were bound to guard with zealous care the sacred deposit of faith which had been committed to their keeping. They knew with infallible certainty that that faith was true —true in substance and true in detail. It had come from the lips of Him who was the Fountain of all truth. They could not allow even the least element of falsehood to be mixed up with it.

They had not been long engaged in the ministry of preaching when they had an opportunity of showing their zeal in protecting it against innovation. The Church was still in her infancy when the voice of error made itself heard, and sought to destroy her young life. Proud, obstinate men arose, who resisted the Apostles, disputed with them, questioned, and even in some points denied, the truth of their teaching. These restless innovators maintained loudly and defiantly that the Gentile converts could not be saved, unless they superadded the observances of the Mosaical Law to those of the New Gospel, and that Judaism was a necessary intermediate step from Paganism to Christianity. St. Paul opposed these positions with all his energy. Peter, James, and John held the same doctrine. The question was one of great moment. The zealots for the Law were moving heaven and earth to carry their point, *i.e.*, to make submission to legal prescriptions a necessary qualification for a Gentile's becoming a Christian. It was a critical time in the life of the Church. The Apostles found themselves placed in circumstances of exceptional difficulty: they must either allow some little falsehood to be mingled with the truths of the Gospel, or they must condemn such falsehood, and condemn it by a public act, which would have the effect of changing into the bitterest enemies of the Church some who had hitherto been most zealous in extending her sway and in propagating her doctrines. They foresaw clearly enough the consequences of such public condemnation. A storm of persecution, which the Church, yet young and, according to human appearances, ill able to bear, was sure to follow. Not merely in Jerusalem and Judea, but in the other Roman provinces—indeed, in every part of the world where Jews were found, it would create bitter and persistent opposition. Perhaps those Jews might prevail so far with the Roman authorities as to induce them to prohibit entirely the further preaching of the New Faith.

Such were the difficulties the Apostles had to contend against—such the dangers they had to encounter. Yet they did not hesitate; they could not allow the Gospel of which they were the appointed guardians to be corrupted, changed, or added to. Compromise in things so sacred was out of the question. There could be no communication between light and darkness; truth and error could not live together in the Church of their Divine Master. They must preserve the deposit of faith pure, integral, incorrupt, unmixed with even the least leaven of falsehood. Though all earth and hell should rage against the rising Church, they must condemn error, condemn it publicly; and condemn it not merely separately and individually, each Apostle by himself—they must condemn it with unanimous voice when met together in sacred council. They were to put on record a public act which would show the people of future times that there was one Gospel, and one only—that it could not change without ceasing to be what it was in the beginning. And the example they were thus to set in the very dawn of Christianity was to be a standing record throughout all centuries and all generations how error was to be treated—how the Gospel of Christ could never bear the innovations of human opinion— how that Gospel, pure, intact, unchanged, as it came from the lips of its Divine Author, was the one to be transmitted to succeeding ages, and not some other gospel that was more or less at variance with it.

Though it was inconvenient at the time to hold a council, yet a council was held. It was the first ever convoked in the Church. All the Apostles who could be present took part in it. Some were far away in distant lands teaching and preaching; one, St. James the Greater, had already received the crown of martyrdom. Peter, James the Less, and John, Paul and Barnabas were there. Peter, as prince of the Apostles, Vicar of Christ, first Pope, opened the council and presided throughout. The doctrines and observances which the innovators sought to introduce were examined, discussed and condemned. All agreed that such doctrines were irreconcilable with the Gospel of their Divine Master. The parting words which that Divine Master had spoken on the day of His Ascension were still fresh in their memories and still sounding in their ears : "Going, teach all nations . . . teaching them to observe all things whatsoever I have commanded you". And the Holy Ghost, who had been promised to the Church, who had already come down into her, and who was to dwell in her to the end of time, was with them to suggest to them all truth. He guided them in their mode of acting, inspired their deliberations, placed the matter in clear light before them, swayed their decision, and left no room for doubt as to the course they must follow. They knew with infallible certainty that the Mosaical prescriptions were not amongst the things which their Divine Master had commanded to be observed; and they knew with equal certainty that that Divine Master would never allow man to add to, or subtract from, or change in any way whatever the Gospel which He had announced. That Gospel was in their hands, and they would guard its identity and integrity at the expense of their lives. They condemned emphatically and unhesitatingly the doctrine which taught the obligation of the Jewish ceremonial law on the Gentile converts.

"Then it pleased the Apostles and ancients, with the whole Church, to choose men of their own company, and to send them to Antioch with Paul and Barnabas: Judas who was surnamed Barsabas, and Silas, chief men among the brethren, writing by their hands: The Apostles and ancients, brethren, to the brethren of the Gentiles that are at Antioch and in Syria and Cilicia, greeting: Forasmuch as we have heard that some who went out from us have troubled you with words, subverting your souls, to whom we gave no commands: it hath seemed good to us, assembled together, to choose out men, and send them to you with our dearly-beloved Barnabas and Paul; men who have given their lives for the name of our Lord Jesus Christ. We have sent, therefore, Judas and Silas, who themselves also will by word of mouth tell you the same things. For it hath seemed good to the Holy Ghost and to us to lay no further burden upon you than these necessary things: that you abstain from things sacrificed to idols, and from blood, and from things strangled, and from fornication: from which things keeping yourselves, you shall do well. Fare ye well" (*Acts* xv. 22-29).

Such was the decree. The importance attached to it, the care that was taken to promulgate it, and the effort that was made to secure its observance, may be judged from the forty-first verse of the fifteenth chapter of the Acts, in which the history of the council is given: "And he (Paul) went through Syria and Cilicia, confirming the Churches: commanding them to keep the precepts of the Apostles and the ancients". And the same may be gathered from the fourth verse of the sixteenth chapter, in which are found these words: "And as they (Paul and Timothy) passed through the cities they delivered unto them the decrees for to keep, that were decreed by the Apostles and ancients who were at Jerusalem".

The consequences they had anticipated quickly followed. Several apostacies date from the holding of that council. Some, who till then had been amongst the most firm adherents of the Church, broke with her completely, and became her most bitter and determined persecutors. As long as she withheld from condemning Judaising innovations, they were numbered amongst her best friends; the moment she pronounced her definition of condemnation, they assumed an attitude of the most desperate antagonism. Her stern, unyielding guardianship of her doctrines brought upon her a persecution from which a slight compromise would have saved her. But she could not purchase peace at the sacrifice of even the least tittle of her teaching.

Now, does not the course of action which this council followed naturally suggest the question: Would the Apostles have acted piously, prudently, or even justly, in thus giving a decision which they foresaw would most likely sever from the Church for ever men who had great influence for good or for evil, if they thought it mattered little whether people believed the Gospel as our Lord delivered it, or believed that Gospel when added to, diminished, or changed by the innovations of man? Or, if they thought it mattered little whether an element of falsehood was mixed up with the truth, why not tolerate the different views prevailing as to the obligation or non-obligation of the Mosaic ceremonial law being essential to the Christian Faith, and leave all in peace and free to hold which opinion they preferred on this point, provided they professed themselves members of the New Church, and continued to fulfil her precepts?

But, further, does not the holding of that council, the circumstances that led to its convocation, and the decisions it put forth, suggest another question? Would those Apostles, who condemned so loudly this innovation of Judaism, have approved the modern system of Liberalism in religion, of Latitudinarianism, of Indifferentism, or whatever other name we choose to give it? Would Peter, James and John, Paul and Barnabas, or any other Apostle, or all the Apostles, have ratified at that council the doctrine that God was indifferent what form of Christian belief people nominally adhered to, provided they were good people after their own fashion? Can any reasonable, serious man hold that the Apostles had it in their power on that occasion to pronounce the decision that, after all, men were not strictly bound to believe the doctrines of the New Gospel—that they were quite at liberty to adopt any other doctrines in preference if they chose? If so, it was useless to hold a council at all, useless to teach, useless to preach; and far worse than useless, it was both indiscreet and foolish to evoke such a storm of opposition to themselves.

A theory of religion that would have been condemned in the Church of the first century cannot be regarded as tenable in the Church of the nineteenth. The Church of Christ does not change—if she did, she would not be the Church of Christ. She cannot condemn a doctrine at one period as heretical, and sanction it at another as being in harmony with orthodox teaching.

Here, then, in the very outset of Christianity, we see the Apostles in possession of the deposit of faith, holding in their hands the treasure of those revealed truths which their Divine Master meant to constitute His religion—a religion which was more precious in their eyes than life itself, and to protect which against the blighting breath of error they were willing to shed their blood and die the martyr's death. Restless, turbulent, novelty-seeking men sought to tear it from their grasp, to enlarge it, to improve it, to make it

square with their individual ideas of Christian obligation, to give it a form of their own ; but an authoritative declaration, which bore upon it the impress of
Divine inspiration, coming from the lips of Apostles
assembled in sacred council, made them understand
that that religion meant *one* thing, and not *anything*—
that it was impenetrable to heresy—that it was proof
against the assaults of error or innovation—that the
opinions of men's private judgment could never find
a place in it—that the privilege of individual preference
must ever be discountenanced and repudiated by it,
as a blasphemous attempt to dissolve the Gospel of
Christ, and to melt to nothing the doctrines He came
from Heaven to announce—that it must ever keep the
form and shape and colour it had at the beginning—
that it must preserve till the end of time the complete
identity it had on the day when it was first confided
to their sacred keeping.

Such was the attitude of the Church towards heresy
and innovation in the first century, while her first
Apostles still lived. She had just come fresh from
the hands of her Divine Founder. The Holy Ghost
had descended upon her on the day of Pentecost, and
she was yet in the splendours of His first indwelling.
The Apostles, who were the custodians of her doctrines,
and who were to bear them to the ends of the earth,
were guided by the inspirations of that Divine Spirit ;
and, thus guided, they acted in the Name and spoke
with the Voice of Him who gave them the great
commission to teach and to preach. What *they*
approved was approved by *Him*, and what *they*

condemned was condemned by *Him*. Surely we cannot say that in preaching the Gospel, and in condemning error, they went beyond the limits of His authorisation. Surely the course of action which they took in the face of heresy was the course of action their successors were to take in similar circumstances to the end of time. Surely, too, all will freely admit that the Church was right in *their* day ; for if she was not right in *their* day she has *never* been right. And if in that day, when, in the admission of all, she had still upon her the signs of her Divine credentials, she was so intolerant of error, can she afford to be less intolerant of error now? If she felt it a duty to condemn error in the first century, can she let it pass unnoticed in the nineteenth? If she would not allow the least addition to be made to her doctrines while her first Apostles still lived to be her mouthpiece, can she allow the people of the present day to make any change in those doctrines, or to believe what they like or deny what they like? If so, who gave her leave to change her spirit—to depart from the stern, unyielding rigour with which she guarded the Gospel of her Divine Founder in the beginning? Who authorised the successors of the Apostles to be more indulgent towards heresy than the Apostles had been themselves? Was the Church which would not, and could not, bear the interference of free inquiry in the apostolic age to set the seal of her sanction on that privilege at any future date? Did she not mean the decisive voice of her first council to give the tone to her teachings in this respect down to the consummation of the world?

Suppose that that first council had been convoked, not to discuss the question of Jewish or Mosaical observances, but to discuss the question which is the main subject of this little tract—*i.e.*, whether one religion was as good as another, whether it could be lawfully held that God did not care what religion people professed, provided they were good people after their own ideas—could we imagine the Apostles putting forth a decision like this?—"Knowing that all religions are equal in the sight of God, and foreseeing the different opinions that will prevail amongst men, and foreseeing, consequently, the difficulty of preserving unity in matters of doctrine, it hath seemed good to the Holy Ghost and to us to declare that all people shall be at perfect liberty to believe that one religion is as good as another—that they shall be at perfect liberty to give any meaning they like to those words of Christ, and to those words of us, the Apostles, which will be handed down to them—that they shall be entirely free, too, to believe as much as they like or as little as they like—that it is a matter of absolute indifference to God what creed a man professes, provided he live up to it".

Now, if the theory of Indifferentism, Latitudinarianism, Liberalism in religion, were tenable, this decision would have sounded perfectly natural on the lips of the Apostles assembled in council; and yet such decision would have been in absolute opposition to the sacred cause that had brought them together, and that united their voices in condemning the men who sought to force upon the Church their own private, personal views of religion. Nay, it would be nothing short of a blasphemy to say that such a definition could come from the lips of those who stood around Jesus Christ on the day of His Ascension and heard from His lips the memorable words—"Going teach all nations . . . teaching them to observe all things whatsoever I have commanded you". May we not imagine we hear those heroic heralds of the faith speaking from the benches of that first council chamber to the generations yet unborn—to their successors in the most distant centuries?—and saying to them—"As *we* have done, so do ye. Guard, protect, defend the deposit of faith against the assaults of innovation, against the dictates of private judgment, against the errors of men, against all the false theories of time, and do not ever allow even the least breath of heresy to rest upon it."

CHAPTER V.

Further Refutation of Indifferentism from Revelation—Refutation from St. Paul's Epistle to the Galatians.

I HAVE said that the importance attached to the decree of the Council of Jerusalem, the care that was taken to promulgate it, and the effort that was made to secure its observance, might be gathered from the forty-first verse of the chapter in which the history of the council is given. Allusion is made in the verse in question to the mission of St. Paul to the churches in Syria and Cilicia: "And he (Paul) went through Syria and

Cilicia confirming the churches; commanding them to keep the precepts of the Apostles and of the ancients".

I may add that the effort made to procure the fulfilment of that decree may be seen in still clearer light in the words of that great Apostle himself to the Galatians. In his epistle to the neophytes of Galatia we find him branding with withering curse those very same errors which he and his brethren in the Apostolate had assembled in council to combat and to crush. And the words of warning and reprehension which he writes on the occasion embody an overwhelming refutation of this flexible system of Indifferentism.

Language could not be stronger, more clear, or more scathing than that in which this great doctor of the Gentiles condemns and anathematises those who sought to introduce a second Gospel among the Galatians. He himself had evangelised the Galatians, and had made them members of the one true fold. Scarcely, however, had the seeds of faith begun to germinate and produce fruit amongst them, when the voice of heresy was heard. Galatia was one of the portions of Asia Minor in which the struggle made by the Jewish converts to have the ceremonial precepts of the Mosaical law superadded to the Gospel of Christ, and made binding on the Gentile converts, was most violent and most persistent. The Judaising teachers had succeeded in spreading their doctrines of innovation pretty widely. St. Paul, hearing that some of those whom he had won to Christ had fallen away, through the influence of spurious evangelists, wrote an epistle to the Galatians. The first chapter of that epistle strikes as directly at certain errors of the present day as at those errors in condemnation of which it was originally written. After wishing the Galatians grace and peace from God the Father and from our Lord Jesus Christ, he says: "I wonder that you are so soon removed from him who called you to the grace of Christ, to another gospel: which is not another; only there are some that trouble you, and would pervert the Gospel of Christ. But though we, or an angel from heaven, preach a gospel to you, beside that which we have preached to you, let him be anathema. As we said before, so I now say again: If any one preach to you a gospel besides that which you have received, let him be anathema. For I give you to understand, brethren, that the Gospel which was preached by me is not according to man. For neither did I receive it from man, nor did I learn it, but by the revelation of Jesus Christ."

I have just implied that this scathing, unqualified condemnation of false teaching strikes as directly at the Indifferentism of the nineteenth century as at the errors of the innovators of the first century, who sought to impose useless burdens on the Galatians. May I not express the idea in stronger language still? St. Paul was denouncing men whose chief error was to put forward as binding in conscience certain ceremonial precepts of the Mosaic Law, which had been of obligation in the Old Dispensation, which could never be binding as part of the New, and which were to be entirely abolished in the first century of the

Church's history. The aim of those proud zealots was not so much to change any particular article of faith, as to add to the articles of faith, superfluous, and henceforth useless, ceremonial observances. And if he spoke with such vehemence against those who tried to add to the Gospel things which had once been obligatory, and still were lawful, for Jewish converts, would he not have used stronger and more unsparing language still, if such could be conceived, against the abettors of a system which attempts to overthrow the fundamental doctrines of Christianity, and which teaches errors which are in open, palpable contradiction to them? If he hurled such withering anathemas on the heads of the men who dared to add human opinions to the doctrines of the Church, what anathemas would he not thunder against those who should seek to sap her very foundations by proclaiming that it did not matter whether people believed the Gospel she taught, or some other Gospel which denied what she affirmed, and affirmed what she denied!

Can we conceive the man who wrote these words of apostolic censure receiving into the Church, or permitting to remain *in* the Church, Galatians, Romans, Corinthians, Ephesians, Philippians, Colossians, Thessalonians, Hebrews, Jews, or people of any country under the sun, if they persisted in refusing to become her members, or to remain in her communion, except on the condition that they were to have the free exercise of their private judgment and to be at liberty to accept or to retain this or that particular doctrine according to their own individual interpretation of what is contained in Holy Scripture? Or can we imagine that if he appeared now in this nineteenth century before the influential, learned advocates of Indifferentism, he would give any assent to, or connive at, the statement that all gospels are good—that one religion is as good as another—that all Christian creeds, although they contradict each other in matters which are of vital importance, if any can be, are equally good, or pretty much the same; and that it is quite immaterial which of them a man embraces as his symbol of faith, provided he shape his life after the one upon which his choice has fallen? *They* must have a strong imagination, indeed, who can suppose that such a theory could be endorsed by the Apostle, who pronounced such scathing anathemas on the innovators of Galatia.

But, further, it must not be overlooked (for it is a point deserving of very special notice) that he expresses his condemnation of those erring evangelists who sought to force false teachings on the Galatians, a second time, and almost in the same terms. Lest the Galatians might suppose that his words of censure were rhetorical, or that he was writing from human impulse, or that he was rebuking them from a feeling of intense disappointment at their sudden change, and that in calmer moments he would reprove them with less severity—lest any thought of that kind should enter their minds, he repeats, with all the power he can command, and with all the emphasis with which his character of Apostle can invest his words, the same anathema again: "As we said before, so I say now again: If any one preach to you a gospel, besides that which you have received, let him be anathema ".

More than this, as the false teachers, whose sophistry and influence he wanted to make powerless, had quoted, but of course falsely quoted, the authority of Peter, James, and John in support of their opinions, he (St. Paul) pointed to the Gospel which he had preached as a thing of such sacredness, such indissoluble unity, such everlasting identity, that neither he nor any of the Apostles, nor even an angel of God, had power to change it in the least item. "I wonder," he says, "that you are so soon removed from him who called you to the grace of Christ, to another gospel, which is not another." He first condescends to style the errors of those heretical evangelists "another gospel," in order that, by correcting himself in having dignified them by that name, he may draw more attention to them, and that his overwhelming, crushing condemnation of them may call forth greater horror, and may be more deeply impressed upon their memories. "Which is not another gospel," he adds; for another gospel there cannot be—there can never be. There is but one, *the* one which we have preached to you—while the world lasts there cannot be another. Wicked men may strive to pervert it, to add to it, to diminish and explain it away, to mutilate, to corrupt, to change it; but it still remains, and must *ever* remain, unchanged, unchanging, and unchangeable, like the God whose immutable truths it announces. "Jesus Christ yesterday, and to-day, and the same for ever" (*Heb.* xiii. 8). "One Lord, one faith, one baptism. One God and Father of all, who is above all, and through all, and in us all" (*Ephes.* iv. 5, 6).

Some, however, who would fain justify, through the principles of Indifferentism, the system of faith which they at present profess (although they have serious misgivings about its truth), take refuge in a fact which affords anything but ground for solid argument. When driven from every other position, they fall back upon this as a sort of forlorn hope. They say: "The creed which I now profess was the creed professed by my father; it was the creed of my grandfather, the creed of my ancestors from time immemorial—at all events, since the Reformation; if it was good enough for them, it ought to be good enough for me".

This is weak philosophy indeed. The many and wonderful conversions to the Catholic faith which have taken place in England within the last half century might be regarded as furnishing a sufficient answer to this. But entirely apart from the logic of such events, an answer is easily found. The fact that a man's religion was the religion of his father, the religion of his grandfather, and the religion of his ancestors for centuries past, does not prove that religion to be true. If it was wrong in its beginning, it has been wrong ever since; age cannot have made it right. The transmission of an error from one generation to another cannot change that error into truth. Length of time, under certain given circumstances, may give a prescriptive claim to the possession of property, but no number of years can give error any sort of claim to the submission of man's understanding. A custom may be sanctified by antiquity; but an antiquity equal to the age of the world could not sanctify falsehood or change heresy into orthodox religion.

That falsehood may be polished up, refurbished, gilded, draped in a fascinating sophistry, which makes it appear tolerable, plausible, and even commendable in the eyes of the over-credulous and unreflecting; it is falsehood, however, all the while, and must remain falsehood to the day of doom.

More than this, if reasoning of this kind justified a man in remaining in the creed he was born in, the Gospel of Christianity could never have been reasonably expected to make any progress. For both the Jews and the Gentiles, to whom the Apostles preached, might, in such a supposition, have rejected entirely the doctrines of the New Faith. They could have said to those who sought to make the light of the Christian Gospel shine upon them that they were quite satisfied with the religion they were already professing, that it had been the traditional religion of their families for centuries before, that they did not deem themselves better than those of their race who had gone before them, and that they could not make up their minds to abandon a form of worship to which their predecessors had clung so long, so faithfully, so persistently, and so scrupulously.

But further, our opponents, by this quasi-appeal to the past, are unconsciously opening the way to the argument which, of all others, is the most fatal to the theory they are advocating. For although their present faith has been, in its many and perpetually changing forms, the faith of their fathers for some generations, or even some centuries past, yet there was a time a little further back when it was not the faith of their fathers. From the sixteenth century, Protestantism, or some fragmentary religion which was an offspring of Protestantism, *may* have been the creed according to which the successive generations of their family worshipped; beyond that century it could not have been, for the simple reason that it did not exist. And if it had no existence till *then*, and was born into the world only at that date, it was born more than fifteen hundred years too late to be the religion of which St. Paul spoke when he said: "If I or an angel of heaven preach to you a gospel besides that which we have preached, let him be anathema".

Cardinal Manning, speaking on "Revealed truth definite and certain," and referring to this last resource of the Indifferentist, says: "Well, you will perhaps tell us that you have inherited the faith you hold. The inheritance of faith, that is a Divine principle. We bow before the principle of inheritance. But why did you cut off the entail of your forefathers? Why, three hundred years ago, did you cut off the entail of that inheritance? If it be not cut off, why is the contest? If it be cut off, why was it cut off? To inherit the faith is the Divine rule. It needs only one thing, infallibility, to secure it. It needs only one support to give it substance and certainty: a Divine tradition flowing from the Throne of God through

Prophets, Seers, Apostles, Evangelists, Martyrs, Saints, and Doctors in one world-wide stream, ever deepening, never changing, from the beginning until now. Show this Divine certainty as the basis of your conviction, and then inherit both truth and faith. But the inheritance of opinion in a family, or a diocese, or a province, or nation—what is it? Human in the beginning, and human to the end: 'the traditions of men'. You say you have inherited the faith, and that this is the Church of your forefathers. Go back three hundred years ago and ask the priests of God, who stood then at the altar, how *they* would expound the faith you still profess to hold. Ask them what they believed while they ministered in cope and chasuble. Go back to the Apostle of England who first bore hither again the light of the Gospel after Saxon paganism had darkened this fair land. Ask St. Augustine what he believed of these words : 'Thou art Peter, and upon this rock I will build My Church'. Give *your* exposition, and ask *his*. What would he have taught you of visible unity? What would he teach you of the Church of God? Ask him: Is it one numerically, or only by metaphor? Is it visible, that all men may see 'the city seated on a mountain,' or invisible, that men may weary themselves and never find it? Has it a head on earth representing its Divine Head in heaven? Or has it no head, and may set up many of its own? What would he have taught you of your baptismal creed? Or that great Saint who sent him from the apostolic throne, what would he have testified to you of those doctrines of

faith which you are to look upon as errors? Ask
Gregory, first and greatest of the name, what he
believed of the powers left by the Incarnate Son to
His Church on earth; what he taught of the power
of the keys transmitted by his predecessors in lineal
descent from the hands of his Divine Lord. Ask
what he taught of the power of absolution in the
Sacrament of Penance; what he believed of the
Reality on the altar, and of the Holy Sacrifice daily
offered in all the world; of the Communion of Saints
ever interceding, by us ever invoked; of the intermediate state of departed souls, purifying for the
kingdom of God. Ask Gregory, saint and doctor,
to whom we owe the faith, what he taught of those
doctrines which you have rejected. If the disciple
and his Master, if he that was sent and He that sent
him, were to come now and tread the shore of this
ancient river, whither would they turn to worship?
Would they go to the stately minster, raised by their
sons in the faith, where even now rests a sainted king
of Catholic England? Would they bend their steps
thither to worship the God of their fathers, and their
Incarnate Lord, from whom their mission and their
faith descended? or would they not rather go to some
obscure altar in its neighbourhood, where an unknown
and despised priest daily offers the Holy Sacrifice in
communion with the world-wide Church of God? If
then you claim inheritance as the foundation of your
faith, be true to your principle, and it will lead you
home. Trifle not with it. Truth bears the stamp of
God, and truth changes men to the likeness of God.

Trifle not with the pleadings of the Holy Spirit within you ; for He has a delicate touch, and sensitively shrinks from wilfulness and unbelief. If truth struggle within you, follow it faithfully. Tread close upon the light that you possess. Count all things loss that you may win truth, without which the inheritance of God's kingdom is not ours. Labour for it and weary your-selves until you find it. And forget not that if your religion be indefinite, you have no true knowledge of your Saviour ; and if your belief be uncertain, it is not the faith by which we can be saved " (*The Grounds of Faith*, pp. 16-19).

Though our proper scope is rigid demonstration, yet we may be excused if we make the following little digression to record an example which bears intimately on the phase of Indifferentism which we have just been noticing. This little book may (and we hope it will, largely) fall into the hands of persons outside the Catholic Church who have begun to doubt the truth of their present religion, and whose chief objection to further inquiry or nearer approach to Catholic unity is the shrinking or shyness, or inward movement of human respect, which they feel at the idea of giving up the traditional creed of their family. Let such reflect on the noble and chivalrous answer given by Count Leopold Stolberg, after he became a Catholic, to Frederick William III., King of Prussia, great-grand-father of the present Emperor of Germany. Stolberg was a man of unswerving uprightness and of uncom-mon learning. He read much, studied much, reasoned much, wrote much and well. All Germany was filled with the fame of his learning, of his writings, and of his high-mindedness. He was a good man according to his lights; he followed those lights faithfully. After mature deliberation, it became clear to him that he was bound to abjure Protestantism and to embrace the Catholic faith in its stead. He did not hesitate or allow himself to be held back by useless and dangerous delays. He made his submission to the Church of Rome promptly and publicly; and did so in spite of difficulties greater in number, and of a more serious kind, than any that surround the conversions which are taking place around us at present. The first time he appeared at court after his renunciation of Lutheranism and solemn reception into the Catholic Church, the king said to him in a tone of bitter reproach: "I cannot respect the man who has abandoned the religion of his fathers". "Nor I, sire," replied Stolberg; "for if my ancestors had not abandoned the religion of *their* fathers, they would not have put *me* to the trouble of returning to it."

Here is the right spirit—here is fearless courage of the right kind. Neither the desire of retaining the king's esteem, nor the fear of losing the king's friendship, could sway this noble-hearted man one iota. He saw that Protestantism meant only Latitudinarianism or Indifferentism, that it had no foundation to rest upon, that it led to incipient Rationalism by bringing revelation down to a level with the law of nature, and that in its further stages it led to Atheism. And, seeing this, he broke with it for ever, and sought admission into the communion of the Church of Rome.

Indifferentism, then, has no firm ground to stand on. It cannot bear investigation. It may appear substantial, firm, fair, and fascinating in the eyes of those who do not care to look beneath the surface; it breaks and crumbles to pieces in analysis.

It would have us believe that God spoke with the view of revealing something, and that yet He revealed nothing definite; that He made known some doctrine, and at the same time gave men leave to give that doctrine any meaning they pleased; that He proclaimed some statement as true, and left men perfectly free to believe it was false; that He made a revelation, and, while making it, did not care in the least in what sense men received it, or whether they received it at all, or whether they received it in two opposite senses, the one contradictory of the other. It would have us believe that, while our Divine Lord says faith is necessary to salvation, faith after all is *not* necessary to salvation; in other words, that the statement is true or false according to the standpoint from which it is looked at. It would have us believe that, while God meant something definite when He gave the Ten Commandments through Moses on Mount Sinai, His Divine Son did not mean anything definite at all when, on the Mount of His Ascension, He commanded His Apostles to teach and to preach to the nations the doctrines and precepts they had heard from Him. It will not allow the Ten Commandments to be subjected to the action of free inquiry or private judgment, and it lets free inquiry and private judgment deal as they like with the doctrines revealed personally, directly, audibly, visibly, by our Lord Himself. It makes the Divine message so impalpable, so versatile, so chameleon-like in its changeableness, that by some inherent, heaven-born property which it possesses, heaven knows how, it necessarily accommodates itself to each fresh mind it meets.

Indifferentism means all this and more. It is a contradiction of man's reason, and it is a contradiction of God's Word. It is a contradiction of the great apostolic commission — "Going, teach all nations, teaching them to observe *all* things whatsoever I have commanded you". It is a contradiction of the teaching of the Holy Ghost, who is the Spirit of truth; for it sanctions contradictory statements, and therefore necessarily sanctions falsehood. It contradicts the collective teaching put forth by the first Apostles in council; for the Apostles met in council expressly to condemn error and to stop the inroads of innovation. It contradicts the teaching of the Apostles taken individually; for St. Paul was only echoing the voice of his apostolic brethren, who had been born into the apostolate before him, when he said: "But though we, or an angel from heaven, preach a gospel to you besides that which we have preached to you, let him be anathema". It is a practical, permanent, persistent contradiction of Christianity. Christianity (I mean orthodox Christianity) may be said to be Christ teaching religion to man. Indifferentism is man explaining *away* that religion, minimising it, reducing it to nothing. Christianity is something supernatural both as to the lights it brings to the mind and as to the laws it imposes on the will. The religion of Indifferentism, when analysed, is hardly anything but an outward, imperfect, and even unfaithful expression of the light of reason, and a repromulgation of the law of nature.

Its natural tendency, therefore (though many of those who profess it as their creed do not, I believe, realise this), is to dissolve all revealed religion, and consequently to dissolve Christ. No creed can stand before so powerful a solvent as this. It is an engine of destruction before which all revealed doctrine must fall to pieces. It tends, as far as in it lies, to loosen every stone in either side of that great arch of Christian truth which spans the universe; nay, it tends to loosen the very keystone of that arch, to bring the whole sacred structure to the ground, to leave the world without a single trace of the Divinity or teaching of Jesus Christ, and to reduce it to that state of spiritual chaos whose only, or whose best, religion is the " Unknowable ". And to this state of utter anarchy in matters of faith, Indifferentism, or Liberalism in religion, would have brought the world long before now, had not the edifice of *true* Christianity been built upon a foundation that could never fail, and been sustained by an omnipotent, though invisible, hand, which made it proof against all the efforts of innovation and all the assaults of men and of devils.

Where that true Christianity is to be found is now the question.

As many of those who belong to non-Catholic denominations will admit that it is *possible at least* that the creed which they now profess is wrong, I do not think that we do any violence to their feelings when we ask them to pray that, in case they have not the true faith at present, the light of God's grace may guide them into the full and calm possession of it. Prayer is the way to the true Church. As the star of the Eastern kings, though its light was intermittent, nevertheless continued to shine with sufficient steadiness till it brought them into the cave of Bethlehem; so the star of grace, which is formed by humble, confident, earnest, and persevering prayer, will infallibly, sooner or later, guide the sincere inquirer into that one true fold in which *alone* Jesus Christ dwells, and in which *alone* He speaks and teaches. It is in the light of this truth we desire all outsiders, into whose hands these pages may fall, to read what we shall now put before them with respect to those signs or marks by which that true fold is to be distinguished from every other. We take the liberty of advising them to ask, in the words of Pope's universal prayer—

" If I am right, Thy grace impart
  Still in that right to stay:
If I am wrong, then guide my heart
  To find that better way ".

PART II.

CHAPTER I.

Unity.

There are many who will accompany us thus far.
They readily grant all that has been said. They
admit that all religions cannot be true—that one only
can be true—that all the rest must be false. They
admit further that there is a true religion in the world
somewhere. This, of course, they are forced to admit ;
else the gates of hell have prevailed, and Jesus Christ
made a promise which He either could not or would
not fulfil. And to say either would be to speak with
grave irreverence against His omnipotence or fidelity.
To assert that He promised to do something which
He did not mean to do, or had not the power to do,
would certainly be a blasphemy.

When at Cesarea Philippi He spoke the memorable
words* in which He proclaimed to the world that
His Church was to be built on a rock, firm, unyielding,
immovable, against which no power of earth or hell
could prevail ; and when again He declared, just

---

* "Thou art Peter ; and upon this rock I will build my
Church ; and the gates of hell shall not prevail against it."—
Matt. xvi. 18.

before ascending to His Father, that He would remain
with her all days until the consummation of the world*
—the whole of her future history was present to Him
—nay, the whole future history of the world, in all
its varied events, circumstances, changes, revolutions,
wars, schemes, intrigues, treasons, schisms, heresies,
stood out as clear before Him as the Apostles whom
He was addressing. For He was God to whose infinite knowledge all things, past, present, and future,
were equally visible. Now, would He, or could He,
have uttered these solemn promises if He had foreseen
there was ever to be a time when His Church would
do any deed, or teach any doctrine, or commit any
betrayal of trust, which would force Him to forsake
her, or force Him to allow the powers of error or of
evil to prevail over her? There is nothing in His
words, nor is there anything in the sacred circumstances
in which He spoke them, to justify any such supposition. His promises are absolute, unconditional, unqualified by any limitation, whether expressed or implied. And surely on such promises we can safely
rest the following statement : The Church of Christ
existed once on earth ; and so surely as she existed
once, so surely does she exist *still*, in some part of the
world or other, else Christ Himself is not God, or if
He is God, He has promised and not fulfilled.

---

* "Going, teach ye all nations ; baptising them in the name of
the Father, and of the Son, and of the Holy Ghost. Teaching
them to observe all things whatsoever I have commanded you,
and behold I am with you all days even to the consummation of
the world."—*Matt.* xxviii. 19, 20.

But now comes the question. The honest, earnest inquirer, who has followed us thus far, will ask: "Which *is* His Church? Where is she to be found? Point her out. Show me how she is to be distinguished amongst the numberless claimants, all of which arrogate to themselves the prerogative of Divine institution. Here I stand," he continues, "bewildered, amid the din, the clash and clamour of contending, antagonistic sects, each and all of which lay claim to truth. Though, in their teachings, they are as far apart from each other as the poles, though they are separated by huge mountains of contradiction, yet they all and each profess to be the true Church. What, then, are the marks, signs, tokens, by which I can find out for certain, and without any lingering feeling of doubt, which amongst them all is the one true Church of Christ?"

Such the question we have to answer. Such our search.

We do not begin by saying which is that Church. We shall come to it step by step. And we shall not seek to advance one inch on the way that leads to our conclusion, except by arguments which we think will be looked upon as honest, fair, straightforward, and solid by all reasonable men.

To determine which Church amongst all is right, we must summon the rival claimants before the bar of plain common sense, and examine which claimant has the best, nay, the *only*, claim to be believed the one true Church of Christ.

It is evident that if Christ established His Church

for the salvation of the people of all time, He could not have made her so obscure, so hidden, so mysterious, that it would take years of historical research, and a thorough knowledge of the Scriptures from Genesis to the Apocalypse, to find her out. If so, she would be for ever beyond the reach of the ignorant and uneducated who would be born without her pale. He must have meant her to be something palpable, tangible, visible, *strikingly* visible, easily discoverable by all who had not yet discovered her; and, also, easily distinguishable from the spurious, schismatical, and heretical sects which He foresaw would in time rise up around her and try to supplant her His design was that she should be like the city built on a hill, as plain to the sight of the unlettered, who would open their eyes and look around them, as to the keen penetrating glance of the scientist. For she could never answer to the purpose of universal salvation for which she was framed, unless her Divine credentials were legible to the poor and the rich, the illiterate and the scholar alike.

What are those credentials or marks?

There are several; but they may be reduced to two. At all events, two will be sufficient for our purpose. Whichever Church is Christ's must have these two; and she *alone* ever *can* have them.

One is the Mark of Unity, the other is the Mark of Universality or Catholicity.

All who belong to any Christian denomination will readily grant that whichever Church is Christ's must necessarily have these marks. Several sectarian denominations recite as their symbol of faith the creed (the Nicene Creed) which enunciates them : " And I believe in *one*, holy, Catholic Church ". But quite independently of that ancient formula, reason enlightened by faith compels us to the conclusions that it must be so.

I. *Unity.*—Whichever Church is Christ's must be one—cannot be two. If she were two, she would not be the one true Church of Christ. This may sound a truism. I mean, if she taught contradictory statements about doctrines of vital importance, she could not be the one true Church of Christ. For, if she taught contradictory dogmas of faith, she must needs teach falsehood ; and Christ, who is the God of Truth, and whose voice speaks in her, cannot teach falsehood. Nor can He dwell, by a perpetual and an abiding presence, in any Church which teaches what is false ; for His abiding presence is an approving presence, and He can never set the seal of His approbation, either explicitly or implicitly, on any doctrine which is opposed to truth.

For a similar reason, she (whichever Church is Christ's) cannot sanction, permit, or tolerate the use of any principle or privilege which, taking men as they are, necessarily leads to contradictions in fundamental matters of faith ; just because she cannot sanction, permit, or tolerate any principle or privilege whose application leads of necessity to falsehood. No reasonable man will hold that she would be Christ's Church if she did. These statements will be equivalent to first principles, in the judgment of all who regard the Church as a work of Divine institution.

If we gainsay them, if we refuse to see them in that light we are unconsciously admitting that her teachings, even before the end of the first century, may have been a chaos of contradictory doctrines, in which it would have been impossible to tell whether the element of truth or the element of falsehood predominated. In fact, to deny them is simply to deny to be a mark of the true Church that unity which Christ Himself expressly declared was to be one of her most distinguishing and most striking marks.

At the Last Supper, towards the end of His parting discourse, He raised His eyes to His eternal Father, and prayed that there might be unity amongst His Apostles, and unity amongst the faithful, who through *their* preaching were to believe in His Gospel. And He not only prayed that unity might bind them all together, but He proclaimed in that very same prayer that He meant that unity to be a proof to the world that *they* were His own flock, and that He Himself had been divinely sent: "And not for them (the Apostles) only do I pray, but for them also who through their word shall believe in Me—that they all may be one, as Thou, Father, in Me, and I in Thee; that they also may be one in Us: *that the world may believe that* Thou hast sent Me" (*John* xvii. 20, 21). Now, would not that prayer have been meaningless if He meant, while He said it, that the Apostles or the faithful, the priests or the people, were to have the free use of a privilege before which all definite revelation would melt away—which would leave them free to give opposite forms to every doctrine He had made known and contradictory interpretations to every word of His which was to remain on record? Or, could He, the God of unchanging truth, ever have put forth that solemn petition to the Father, if He intended, while He said it, that Peter was to be free to preach one doctrine in Antioch, and John the contradictory in Ephesus?

Well, I think we may say that two points have been established: 1st, the Church of Christ—the Church of the everlasting rock—exists somewhere on earth; 2nd, that Church can neither teach contradictory doctrines of faith; nor can she approve or tolerate a principle the use of which necessarily leads to contradictions in doctrines of fundamental importance.

Now, apply this test to the numberless creeds outside the Catholic communion which proclaim themselves orthodox, and see if they can stand it.

The principle of private judgment, free inquiry, individual preference, as we shall see presently, not merely leads, but, taking men as they are, leads of *necessity*, to contradictions, and to contradictions in *even* the most important matters of faith; and, consequently, leads of necessity to false conclusions with regard to the most important matters of faith.

But the Church of England, and all the branch Churches which have sprung from her, enforce, sanction, or tolerate the use of private judgment. This statement may sound too bold and comprehensive. It is, however, undeniable. Nearly all the members of the Anglican Communion will admit it; and the twentieth of those Articles on which the Anglican creed is founded plainly professes it. And even the High Church and Ritualistic party, which is loudest in disclaiming it, uses it, and uses it in its most intense form; while those who belong to the Low Church and Broad Church party will not pretend to deny that the Scripture is their only rule of faith, and that private judgment is its interpreter. Besides, those Articles, to which all the clergy of the Establishment are bound to subscribe, are forthcoming to prove that it is so.

In the sixth Article it is stated: "Holy Scripture containeth all things necessary to salvation; so that whatever is not read therein, nor may be proved thereby, is not to be required of any man that it should be believed as an article of faith, or be thought requisite or necessary to salvation". And the twentieth Article runs thus: "The Church hath power to ordain rights and ceremonies, and authority in controversies of faith; and yet it is not lawful for the Church to ordain anything contrary to God's Word written; neither may it so expound any passage of Scripture so as to be repugnant to another".

Dr. Beveridge, a celebrated Protestant divine, whose teaching is confirmed by other and later writers, guided by these Articles, maintains that each individual is bound to look to the proofs of what he specifically believes, and obliged to be a member of his Church on grounds which he himself has verified.

Further remarks on this point are unnecessary, since the principle that each individual must judge for himself, and make out his own system of faith from the

Scriptures, is admitted by the members of the Low Church and Broad Church party.

But even the members of the High Church and Ritualistic party, who will not allow themselves to be reproached with professing the principle of private judgment, use it, and use it, as I have said, in its most exaggerated form.

I will here give my reasons for saying so. Their belief in the past, their change of belief, their present anomalous position, the various phases through which their creed has passed, their stopping within the boundary line which they have now reached, their obstinate unwillingness to move an inch beyond it, make this clear to evidence. Their gradual approach to that series of dogmas, which they at present profess, has been an exercise of private judgment all along. For if, when the hour of change came, they departed from the doctrines of their earlier years, and replaced them by doctrines taught by the Church of Rome, was it not free inquiry, individual preference, and private judgment pure and simple, that led them to take that course? Their interpretation of their Anglican position, and of the formularies and doctrines of their Church, in a Catholic sense, as contrary to the Protestant sense, which had before so long prevailed— what was all that but the result of private judgment? And their standstill on the line of demarkation which now separates them on one side from their co-religionists, and on the other from the members of the Roman Catholic communion—what is it but a constant, continuous exercise of the same arbitrary choice? If they move neither backward towards the creed of their early youth, nor forward still nearer to the Church of Rome, it is nothing but private judgment that keeps them where they are. There is no external power, no authoritative tribunal, to keep them there. Their own Church—the Church to which they nominally belong—is quite passive in their regard. She merely looks upon their state of oscillation, transition, change, with the eye of toleration. And *they* give pretty clear proof that they would not listen to her voice, even if she spoke in the tone of authoritative prohibition. They acknowledge no living authority of any kind which can bind them to keep fixedly to the doctrines which make up their present creed. The only real, living, tangible authority they recognise is their own freedom of mind, individual preference, private judgment, which has been their guide throughout, and which, from the day it broke loose from the traditional fragments of Anglican belief, has never submitted to any external control. And that private judgment, being still free to roam unchecked, being at perfect liberty to change its former decision in a moment, may induce them in the not far distant future to discard utterly all the Catholic doctrines which they at present profess.

They may tell us loudly that they do not use private judgment in the interpretation of the Scripture. Well, if they do not pretend to interpret the Scriptures by private judgment, they interpret the Ancient Fathers by private judgment, and that comes pretty much to the same thing. Perhaps it is more correct to say that they use private judgment in their interpretation both of the Scriptures and of the Fathers. The field in which they exercise private judgment is in reality broader and wider than that claimed by any other sectaries whatever. While others are content to confine the exercise of this arbitrary right to the Bible, *they* let it loose upon the decisions of the early Councils and the writings of the Fathers. That is, they make certain passages of Scripture give out certain favourite doctrines by an appeal to the interpretations given to those passages by the early Fathers; while, with regard to other passages, they reject entirely the interpretations of those Fathers, and follow their own interpretations in preference. If this is not private judgment, it is hard to say what is. They take up the history of the early Councils and the writings of the Ancient Fathers, and they find that the primitive Church must have believed this doctrine, and that doctrine and that other doctrine. Guided by these venerated records, they give to certain passages in Scripture the Catholic interpretation—an interpretation which the other members of their communion entirely disclaim, and emphatically repudiate. They copy these doctrines into their new creed, just because, in their present temper of mind, such doctrines commend themselves to their private fancy.

Then, suddenly, it is found they are prepared to go only a certain length, and no further, with the early Fathers; although there is quite as much reason, and more, for going the whole way, than there is for stopping when they have got a certain distance.

While they gladly transfer into their new symbol of faith the doctrine of Confession and of the Eucharist, because they find these doctrines clearly enunciated in the writings of the Ancient Fathers, they sedulously keep out of it other doctrines of equally vital importance, and which are expressed with equal clearness by the very same Fathers. If they profess to believe that the priest has power to forgive sin, and that Christ is really present in the Eucharist, on the ground that the early Fathers taught these dogmas, why refuse to believe those very same Fathers, when they teach, with equal clearness and equal emphasis, the necessity of being in communion with the See of Rome, and of submitting to its authority, as being an authority which all are bound to obey, and from which there is no appeal? If they agree with St. Irenæus, when he speaks words which embody the Catholic doctrine of the real presence of Christ in the Eucharist, why not agree with the same Irenæus when he teaches so unequivocally that it is necessary that every Church should be in communion with the Church of Rome? No words could be clearer than those which this Father of the Church uses when referring to this vital doctrine :—

" For with this Church " (the Church of Rome), " on account of a more powerful principality, it is necessary that every Church, that is, the faithful on every side, should meet together, in which Church has ever been preserved that tradition which is from the Apostles " (*Adv. Hær.*, Lib. iii., c. 3).

What reason can they give for taking in just so

much of the dogmatic teaching of the primitive
Church as they do take in, and nothing more, and for
treating all the rest as a matter of comparatively
trivial importance?

Is it not evident that although they borrow certain
materials from the early Church in building up their
creed, they are *not* following her teachings, but rather
the dictates of their own private judgment, and the
promptings of their own imagination?

While they disobey the traditions of the Establishment by embracing a belief rejected by most of its
Bishops and the greater part of its laity, they at the
same time refuse to obey any other Church, except
that ideal one which exists in their own imagination,
and can exist nowhere else. I say it can exist nowhere
else; for no Church such as they picture to themselves ever came into actual life. The ancient one, of
which they pretend theirs is the modern realisation or
semi-miraculous resurrection, was in communion with
Rome. If, then, they mean theirs to be the identical
ancient Church, it must have the Roman Pontiff for
its head; and since it has not the Roman Pontiff for
its head, but is a body or part of a body without a
head at all, it cannot be the identical old Church.

Their Church is a nebula—it is a structure in the
air. It is not God's work, it is their own work—a
thing struck out of their own head, created, framed
in outline, and decorated in detail by the exercise of
private judgment and the caprice of individual taste.
Trace the process they follow in its formation, and
you will find this to be the case. They draw a plan

in their mind of what they imagine the ancient Church must have been, then they gather fragmentary or isolated doctrines from the early chronicles of the Church of the East and of the West, from the writings of the ancient Latin Fathers and of the ancient Greek Fathers; they introduce a sprinkling of the novelties of the Reformation; they also draw upon certain doctrines of their own invention; and out of these heterogeneous elements they rear their phantom fabric.

Their religion, then, as it exists in its present form, is entirely their own arbitrary creation. It owes its whole being to the activity of private judgment. Hence, *they* are not under *its* control; *it* is entirely under *their* control. They made it when they chose; they can keep it for as long or as short a time as they choose; they can abolish it any moment they deem it prudent or expedient to do so. It was private judgment that called it into being; the same private judgment can annihilate it in the twinkling of an eye.

In other words, the Church they profess to belong to is either dead or living. If it is dead it cannot receive their submission, and they cannot obey it. If it is living, it must be the primitive Church *out* and *out* or it is nothing. Else they must have us believe that the pure, perfect, primitive Church died and disappeared altogether from history for centuries; that the very rock moved away out of sight too; and that that ancient rock and ancient Church, in all its beauty, perfectness, and completeness, emerged from chaos about the middle of the nineteenth century, and reappeared in themselves in the form of High-Churchism and

Ritualism. And this, I think, is rather an extravagant and unwarrantable supposition.

It is hard indeed to conceive how the mere fact of arbitrarily taking up a certain number of doctrines can reach over a dead past of 1500 or at the least 1000 years, and connect them with a Church which lived only during the three first centuries, or, at the longest, only till the Photian Schism in the ninth century, and which died and was buried then, and has lain buried ever since. What proof can they give, that the act of reading a new profession of faith, or a mere volition, can restore a dead Church to life?

By holding any such theory, they virtually claim the credit of having worked a greater miracle than the resurrection of Lazarus. Lazarus had been only the fourth day in the tomb, when, at the bidding of our Divine Lord, he rose to life.

Ritualists would have us believe that their forming themselves into a distinct religious body, of which nothing has ever been heard before, has produced the twofold wonderful effect—of bringing back to life a Church that had been dead for centuries, and of making them, in the very same instant, members of it.

It is in vain, however, they will strive to stretch over a gulf of 1500 or 1000 years and ask to shake hands with Augustine, or Athanasius, Cyril, Ambrose, or Jerome, with the hope they will be recognised by those early heroes of the faith as members of the same communion.

Were those great doctors to return again to life, doubtless they would tell them, that while they were willing enough to stretch out to them the hand of charity, yet they could never look upon them as members of the same Church, so long as they did not obey one central, unfailing authority, from which there was no appeal.

The members of the Ritualistic Communion may say that they believe all the Catholic doctrine, and that entering into the Roman Catholic Church would not add anything to their creed, except the dogma which teaches that the Pope has universal spiritual jurisdiction over the whole earth. I answer *that* is an essential point.

"Never," says Cardinal Wiseman, "were men more slightly separated from the acknowledged truth than were the Samaritans in the time of our Lord. . . . Slight as were the dissenting principles of those sectarians, amiable and charitable as may have been their characters, ripe as they were for Christianity, affable and conciliating as the interview (with the Samaritan woman) had hitherto been, no sooner is this important question put, than He makes no allowance, no compromise, but answers clearly and solemnly: 'Salvation is of the Jews'. . . . Thus did this benign and charitable Saviour, who came to seek and save what was lost, and whose first principle it was: 'I will have mercy and not sacrifice'—thus did He hesitate not a moment to pronounce, in the clearest terms, that no deviation from the true religion, however trivial, can be justified or excused in His sight" (*Lecture on the Catholic Church*, pp. 326-328).

The Church of England then in all its schools of

opinion—High Church, Low Church, Broad Church—
with the numberless subdivisions of these great parties,
enforces, sanctions, permits, or tolerates the use of
the privilege of private judgment in the interpretation
of the Scripture.

But the use of private judgment, in the interpretation
of the Scripture, leads necessarily (taking men as they
are) to contradictions in matters of faith, and consequently leads necessarily to falsehood in matters of
faith.

The very meaning of private judgment as a privilege or principle makes this sufficiently clear. What
is its meaning? When analysed, it plainly means that
a number of men, say twenty, may open the Bible,
take any verse of it they like, and may, each of them,
give to that verse the interpretation his individual
judgment dictates—the meaning which commends
itself most to his particular judgment or taste. Now,
men differ in temper of mind, in intellect, in disposition, in character, in education, in convictions, prejudices, leanings, inclinations. A hundred contingencies
will influence the meaning they give to the verse in
question. The inevitable result of this exercise of
liberty will be that, in many cases, one man will give
to that verse one interpretation, another will give it an
interpretation absolutely contradictory; and each of
them, thus using the privilege his Church so freely
allows him, maintains that *his* view of the matter is
quite as likely to be correct as that taken by his
neighbour, who gives the inspired words a meaning
totally opposite. And really, looking at the thing

from *his* standpoint, it is hard to blame him. For if inspiration, as his Church represents, is abundantly vouchsafed to individuals, he cannot see why *he* may not claim as large a measure of it as his friend, whose life, as far as *he* can perceive, is not more edifying than his own. Enjoying this fulness of unrestricted freedom, there is nothing to prevent them from differing on every single verse from Genesis to the Apocalypse. And what is more, there is no guarantee that they will agree even in their interpretation of those passages which have reference to the most vital doctrines of Christianity. There is no magisterial authority to bring their minds into oneness of thought. They recognise no superior control which can adjust their differences; nor does their Church oblige them to recognise any. For, in the twentieth Article in which it is stated that she has authority in matters of controversy; in the very same clause, it is implied that she is fallible, and quite as liable to err as the least individual who belongs to her communion; nay, it is implied that the individual has a right to sit in judgment upon her, and to decide whether she ordains anything contrary to God's word written, or whether she expounds one verse of Scripture so as to be repugnant to another. She herself does not claim to have a definite voice; nor does she point to any higher or supreme tribunal from which there is no appeal. Her children are left free to believe that she may go as deeply into error, in the interpretation of the Scriptures, as the most ignorant and least instructed amongst themselves. She may refer them in their controversies to the Sovereign as her head, or to the Privy Council as the organ of her voice; but in doing so the hopes of obtaining certainty do not become greater. It is one fallible individual appealing to another equally fallible, or to a tribunal consisting of fallible individuals, all of whom, collectively, admit that their united decision may be as far away from the truth, as if it was given separately and individually by each, when a thousand miles away from his fellow-councillor.

It is of no use to say that the highest court of appeal in the Church of England never erects itself into a standard with regard to matters of faith, or presumes to decide on such matters—that it itself appeals to the received formularies of the Anglican Church, and that the most it does is to decide whether some disputed doctrine is opposed to, or is in accordance with, these formularies.

Even so, it formally and authentically interprets them; and, while doing so, admits, at least implicitly, that the interpretation may be wrong, since it does not claim to be infallible—nay, admits that the very Articles themselves may be full of error, since they were drawn up by fallible men, men who never claimed, professed, or pretended to be *infallible*. For, after all, *what are these formularies?* Which is this standard itself, to which all in the Anglican Communion, High, Low, and Broad, must bow? What but the teachings and decisions of the English Protestant Reformers of the sixteenth and seventeenth centuries, who can claim no more gift of inerrancy, or an effusion of the Holy

Ghost, than the divines of the nineteenth century: fallible men who severed themselves from the traditional teaching of their forefathers, and from communion with Rome. It is hard to discover any theological or solid reason why the dicta of fallible men, who lived three centuries ago, should continue to be the fixed standard of doctrine for Anglicans in the present century.

With such unlimited liberty, then, as the Church of England allows, in sanctioning the use of private judgment, there may be as many contradictory meanings of Scripture as there are individuals who can read its pages, and consequently as many contradictory creeds.

Such is private judgment. Such it is, such it has been, such it ever *must* be, and such the fatal consequences to which it must necessarily lead. Whether it is gilded by the softer and more refined names of free inquiry, individual preference, liberty of opinion, freedom of thought, the meaning is the same, and the same inevitable results follow from its application.

The use, therefore, of private judgment in the interpretation of the Scripture necessarily leads to contradictions in matters of faith, and to contradictions in matters of faith of the most momentous importance.

Let us look at the thing in practice. See what is going on around us. The High Churchman takes out of a certain passage in the New Testament the doctrine that Christ is truly and objectively present in the Eucharist; the Low Churchman interprets the same passage to mean nothing more than a figurative and indefinite presence of our Lord in that mystery, through the faith of the receiver. The Ritualist holds that the words of our Lord recorded in the twentieth chapter of St. John's Gospel, "Receive ye the Holy Ghost," &c., prove clearly the power to absolve from sin; his Protestant co-religionist, who has not advanced so far on the road of change, and who still clings to the vague doctrines of Low-Churchism, loudly assert that our Lord's words do not prove that power.

Now, surely if any questions of doctrine, in the sphere of religion, ought to be regarded as supremely important in the eyes of man, these ought. No questions in life can be more closely connected with the sanctification and the ultimate salvation of man's soul, than the true worship of God, and the right use of Christ's ordinances. And yet, on these most vital points, men who profess to belong to the same Church, and who fill her highest offices, using their right of private judgment, give absolutely contradictory interpretations to the passages of Scripture which have reference to them.

Hence the almost measureless doctrinal differences, which separate the various parties of which that Church is now composed. Some with firm conviction believe the Catholic doctrine of the Real Presence; others reject it as intolerable idolatry. Some proclaim their belief in sacramental absolution, and express their astonishment that they could have lived so long and read the Scriptures so often without believing it; others repudiate it with horror and disgust, and designate it as the pest of society.

Now, I ask, has the Church which sanctions a

principle which necessarily leads to such interminable contradictions, and, therefore, to interminable error, any right to be considered the one true Church of Christ? Can any reasonable man, who seriously thinks on the matter, hold that Christ meant to leave to His Church the free use of a principle, prerogative, privilege, which would reduce His religion to a Babel of contradictory opinions? Should any one hold this, he must be prepared to accept the necessary logical conclusion, which is this: that when He (Christ) gave to His Apostles the great commission to preach His gospel to the nations, He authorised Peter to preach the doctrine of the Real Presence in Antioch, authorised John to preach the contradictory in Ephesus, authorised James to preach both the one and the other in Jerusalem—nay, left each Apostle free to affirm that dogma emphatically, and to deny it quite as emphatically, while preaching the very same sermon to the very same audience. And these are conclusions from which these very advocates of private judgment must shrink with horror, if they have any regard for consistency and truth.

If, then, unity is an essential mark of the one true Church of Christ, the Church of England, in her various sections, must give up all claim to Divine institution. For unity she has *not*, has never had, and never *can* have. If unity of doctrine were not something entirely beyond her control, why should there have been in the past, and why should there be in the present, so many different parties holding opposite opinions on the most momentous matters of revelation; all of them, we must remember, tolerated, and mutually tolerating one another, as recognised parties in the same communion; each and all claiming a common right to hold their place, as representing the varied multiform views of one and the same comprehensive Anglican Church? But she does not profess to have it. So far from having any principle that can be a bond, a guarantee, a preservative, a protection of unity, she asserts a principle which makes unity an impossibility. And the history of her variations in the past, her present actual state, the numberless divisions into which she has been torn, are striking illustrations of the disintegrating power of her principle. All these things furnish tangible and irresistible proof that identity of doctrine can never live side by side with the unrestricted use of the privilege of free inquiry.

Let us take some facts from history. Protestantism was not seventy years old when it was divided into two hundred and seventy sects.

Staphylus and Cardinal Hosius counted two hundred and seventy branches of it before the end of the sixteenth century.

Calvin, secretly lamenting the wreck the Reformation had made of Christian unity, wrote to Melancthon that he was anxious to hide, as far as possible, the hideous spectacle of their interminable divisions from the gaze of the world, and particularly from the eyes of future generations. "It is of great importance," he says, "that the divisions which subsist among us should not be known to future ages; for nothing can be more ridiculous than that we, who have been compelled to make a separation from the whole world, should have agreed so ill amongst ourselves from the very beginning of the Reformation" (*Epist.* 141).

Beza wrote to Dudith in the same tone: "Our people," he says, "are carried away by every wind of doctrine. If you know what their religion is to-day, you cannot tell what it may be to-morrow. In what single point are those Churches, which declared war against the Pope, united amongst themselves? There is not one point which is not held by some of them as an article of faith, and by others rejected as an impiety" (Theod. Beza, *Epist. ad Aud. Dudit*).

Melancthon was quite as loud in his lamentation over the Babel of discordant creeds generated by the doctrines of the Reformers as either of the two whom I have quoted: "The Elbe," he says, "with all its waters, could not furnish tears enough to weep over the miseries of the distracted Reformation" (*Epist.*, lib. ii., ep. 202).

But to come to a later date—to our own time. Leslie acknowledges that the character, nature, and principle of private judgment is to produce variety and difference of opinion, and even civil and general war. How great and multiform that variety is—how wide that difference—is abundantly demonstrated in *Whitaker's Almanac* for the year—1893. In page 249 we find that places for religious worship in England and Wales have been certified to the Registrar-General on behalf of over 267 different sects. The list is alphabetical; it begins with the Advent Christians and ends with the Young Women's Christian Association * : very nearly all these sects have had their origin in the errors of the Reformation.

Lord Macaulay, in his essay on Mr. Gladstone's volume, *The State in its Relations with the Church*, makes various allusions to this matter. I wish to reproduce some of them here, because they reveal the very noticeable absence (if I may so speak) from the Church of England of all unity of doctrine, and of every principle that tends to secure or protect unity. His words are particularly remarkable for various reasons : 1st, because they show that unity of faith and private judgment are utterly irreconcilable ; 2nd, while he points to the endless contradictions which private judgment generates, he at the same time asserts that there is no visible body on the face of the earth to whose decrees men are bound to submit their judgment on points of faith—which is equivalent to saying that no Church was instituted by Christ, or that if a Church was instituted by Him, that Church does not exist now ; 3rd, because he is arguing against Mr. Gladstone, whose contention in the volume alluded to is, that unity is essential to truth, and that that unity is a characteristic mark of the Church of England. That unity is essential to truth, Macaulay freely admits ; but he denies loudly that unity is a characteristic mark of the Church of England.

Before adducing from his essay the citations which I wish to insert here, I think it advisable to observe,

* It will be observed that the same religious body or denomination is in some instances variously described.

that my great wonder has been that a man of such
giant intellect as Mr. Gladstone * could have failed
to see that the Church of England, so far from
having unity as her distinctive mark, is, on the contrary, founded on a principle which places it entirely
and for ever beyond her reach—that he could have
failed to see through the shallowness of the sophistry,
with which she must be bolstered up, so as to make
her position plausible, reasonable, tolerable, in the
eyes of the public—and that he could persist in
claiming for her an exemption from error, which she
has never had the boldness to attempt to claim for

* I could have wished that the volume which called forth the
essay in question had not been written by Mr. Gladstone, or
that if such a book were to be written at all, it should have
borne some other name.

I quite endorse the opinion expressed by a great statesman on
the occasion of Mr. Gladstone's recent retirement from the
Premiership,—which was to this effect, namely : that his
(Mr. Gladstone's) was the most brilliant intellect that had been
placed at the service of the State since Parliament began.

My great admiration of Mr. Gladstone's truly transcendent
powers makes me unwilling to speak of his arguments and
inferences in reference to a subject in which both arguments and
inferences are undoubtedly illogical, and must therefore be unhesitatingly condemned.

I am confident, however, that Mr. Gladstone himself would be
the last to blame me for vindicating what I feel convinced to be
the truth, the whole truth, and nothing but the truth.

I must add that it is due to Mr. Gladstone that I should remark,
that, having read the original—*i.e.*, Mr. Gladstone's book—*The
State in its Relations with the Church*—I do not think
Macaulay quotes him fairly in *some* points.

He quotes him fairly, however (so far as I can make out), in
the paragraphs or citations which are noticed in this little
volume.—AUTHOR.

herself. There are others who share this feeling of wonder. Macaulay himself, who, I venture to say, was at all times of his life much more widely separated from Catholic truth than Mr. Gladstone, expresses more than once his unqualified surprise that so clever and clear-sighted a man could claim unity for a Church which is notorious for discords, disagreements, differences ; within whose pale " multitudes of sects are battling," or could think it possible that the use of private judgment or free inquiry could produce or lead to unity of doctrine. He analyses Mr. Gladstone's reasoning on the relations between identity of faith and the use of private judgment. And we think the candid, unprejudiced reader must admit that he does so justly and fairly in the main.

" Mr. Gladstone," he says, " dwells much on the importance of unity in doctrine. ' Unity,' he says ' is essential to truth.' And this is most unquestion-able. But when he goes on to tell us that this unity is the characteristic of the Church of England, that she is one in body and in spirit, we are compelled to differ from him widely. The apostolical succession she may have or may not have ; but unity she most certainly has NOT, and never has had. It is a matter of perfect notoriety that her formularies are framed in such a manner as to admit to her highest offices men who differ from each other more widely than a very High Churchman differs from a Roman Catholic, or a very Low Churchman from a Presbyterian ; and that the general leaning of the Church, with respect to some important questions, has been sometimes one way and sometimes another. Take, for example, the questions agitated between the Calvinists and the Armenians. Do we find in the Church of England with respect to those questions that unity which is essential to truth? Was it ever found in the Church? Is it not certain that at the end of the sixteenth century the rulers of the Church held doctrines as Calvinistic as ever were held by any Cameronian, and not only held them, but persecuted everybody who did not hold them? And is it not equally certain that the rulers of the Church have, in very recent times, considered Calvinism as a disqualification for high preferment, if not for holy orders? . . . It is notorious that some of her most distinguished rulers think this latitude a good thing, and would be sorry to see it restricted in favour of either opinion. And herein we most cordially agree with them. But what becomes of the unity of the Church, and of that truth to which unity is essential? . . .

"What wide differences of opinion respecting the operation of the sacraments are held by bishops, doctors, presbyters of the Church of England, all men who have conscientiously declared their assent to her Articles! . . . Here, again, the Church has not unity, and as unity is the essential condition of truth, the Church has not truth. . . . Nay, take the very question which we are discussing with Mr. Gladstone— To what extent does the Church of England allow of the right of private judgment? What degree of authority does she claim for herself in virtue of the apostolical succession of her ministers? Mr. Gladstone, a very able and a very honest man, takes a view of this matter widely differing from the view taken by others whom he will admit to be as able and as honest as himself. People who altogether dissent from him on this subject eat the bread of the Church, preach in her pulpits, dispense her sacraments, confer her orders, and carry on that apostolical succession, the nature and importance of which according to him they do not comprehend. Is this unity? Is this truth?

" It will be observed that . . . the religion of the Church of England is so far from exhibiting that unity of doctrine which Mr. Gladstone represents as her distinguishing glory, that it is, in fact, a bundle of religious systems without number. It comprises the religious system of Bishop Tomline, and the religious system of John Newton, and all the religious systems which lie between them. It comprises the religious system of Mr. Newman, and the religious system of the Archbishop of Dublin, and all the religious systems which lie between them. All these different opinions are held, avowed, preached, printed, within the pale of the Church, by men of unquestionable integrity and understanding. Do we make this diversity a topic of reproach to the Church of England? Far from it. We would oppose with all our power every attempt to narrow her basis. . . . But what becomes of all Mr. Gladstone's eloquent exhortations to unity? Is it not mere mockery to attach so much importance to unity in form and name, when there is so little in substance —to shudder at the thought of two Churches in alliance with one State, and to endure with patience the spectacle of a hundred sects battling within one Church? And is it not clear that Mr. Gladstone is bound on all his own principles to abandon the defence of a Church in which unity is *not* found?"

The eloquent essayist discusses also the peculiar views held by Mr. Gladstone with respect to private judgment :—

"Mr. Gladstone pronounces the right of private judgment, as it is generally understood throughout Europe, to be a monstrous abuse. He declares himself favourable, indeed, to the exercise of private judgment after a fashion of his own. We have, according to him, a right to judge all the doctrines of the Church of England to be sound, but not to judge any of them to be unsound. He has no objection, he assures us, to active inquiry into religious questions. On the contrary, he thinks such inquiry highly desirable, as long as it does not lead to diversity of opinion ; which is much the same thing as if he were to recommend the use of fire that will not burn down houses, or of brandy that will not make men drunk. He conceives it to be perfectly possible for mankind to exercise their intellects vigorously and freely, on theological subjects, and yet to come to exactly the same conclusion with each other and with the Church of England. And for this opinion he gives, as far as we have been able to discover, no reason whatever, except that everybody who vigorously and freely exercises his understanding on Euclid's theorems assents to them. Everybody, he says, who freely inquires agrees with Euclid ; but the Church is as much in the right as Euclid ; why, then, should not every free inquirer agree with the Church?"

This reasoning is evidently sophistical. For, from the very fact that free inquiry has been allowed, there are opposite creeds in the Church of England, and, the free inquirer does not know which creed is right or which represents most faithfully the teaching of that Church; 2nd, because, having the privilege of free inquiry, he may judge that the Church ordains something contrary to God's written word and expounds some passage of Scripture so as to be repugnant to another; 3rd, because, in the exercise of searching and energetic inquiry, he is free to arrive at the conclusion that the Church is not in the right at all, but is entirely in the wrong. That is, while still remaining a Protestant, he is free to deny entirely or to doubt seriously the minor of the syllogisms to which Macaulay reduces Mr. Gladstone's reasoning—*i.e.*, "The Church is as much in the right as Euclid". Quite consistently with the principle of Protestantism, he may accept all the doctrines of the Catholic Church, even the Pope's universal spiritual jurisdiction included.

Macaulay, after using some illustrations, proceeds: "*Our* way of ascertaining the tendency of free inquiry is simply to open our eyes and look at the world in which we live; and there we see that free inquiry on mathematical subjects produces unity, and that free inquiry on moral subjects produces discrepancy. There would undoubtedly be less discrepancy if inquirers were more diligent and more candid. But discrepancy there will be amongst the most diligent and candid as long as the constitution of the human mind and the nature of moral evidence continue unchanged. That we have not freedom and unity together is a very sad thing ; and so it is that we have not wings. But we are just as likely to see the one defect removed as the other. . . . There are two intelligible and consistent courses which may be followed with respect to the exercise of private judgment : the course of the Romanist, who interdicts private judgment because of its inevitable inconveniences, and the course of the Protestant, who permits private judgment, in spite of its inevitable inconveniences. Both are more reasonable than Mr. Gladstone, who would have private judgment *without* its inevitable inconveniences.

We share the feeling of wonder expressed by Lord Macaulay that a man of Mr. Gladstone's powers can hold that unity is essential to truth, and hold at the same time that unity is the characteristic mark of the Church of England, while that Church permits a principle which necessarily and in point of fact leads to contradictions in the most fundamental doctrines of revelation. Nothing can account for this anomaly except that great natural ability, amounting to genius of even the highest order, is one thing, and supernatural faith is quite another.

We agree with Lord Macaulay again in the inference he draws from his analysis of Mr. Gladstone's theory— namely, " Is it not clear that Mr. Gladstone is bound, on all his own principles, to abandon the defence of a Church in which unity is not found ? "

These quotations strengthen more and more our

thesis, that nowhere in the Church of England is found the mark of unity; and that consequently neither the Church of England, nor any school of opinion in her, can represent the one true Church of Christ. And what we say of the Church of England, with respect to this point, applies equally to all dissenting Churches.

But why use further arguments in *words*? Is not the logic of facts sufficient to prove the point? Look at the Church of England in her present actual state. Some of those who subscribe to her Articles profess all the doctrines taught by the Catholic Church, except the supreme universal spiritual jurisdiction of the Pope over the world. They profess to hold the real presence, transubstantiation, sacramental confession, the sacrifice of the Mass, Purgatory, the invocation of Mary and of the Saints, and nearly all the other doctrines that are contained in the Roman Catholic creed. Others reject all these doctrines as damnable superstition. Now, by what effort of the mind can these two parties be said to be one? By what process of reasoning can it be established that the Church which allows such contradictions to be professed within her pale is one? On what principle can it be said that she has that unity which is essential to truth? What idea can we have of falsehood if we hold that the Church of England is true—is the one true Church of Christ?

But this want of unity is common not merely to all branches of the Church of England; it is common to all religious bodies outside the Church of Rome. As unity cannot be found in any heretical Church, so neither can it be found in any schismatical Church. The Oriental schismatical Churches cannot pretend to possess it. They have always been willing to sacrifice unity of creed to "State" expediency. They do not aim, and cannot aim, at anything higher than material or political unity. On the same principle that Photius and Michael Cærularius broke with Rome, and denied the supremacy of the Roman Pontiff, so the Bishops of those schismatical Churches may, either individually or collectively, sever their connection with their respective patriarchates, deny entirely the authority of their respective patriarchs, and form themselves into distinct and separate religious bodies.*

As a matter of fact, schism has already produced its inevitable consequences in those regions of the East which are still under its sway. It is well known that the Russian Church is undermined throughout her length and breadth by sects which, at the present moment, number the greater part of the population— sects, too, which are filled with the most desperate hatred towards both imperial and patriarchal jurisdiction. There are few who have not heard that the late Czar Nicholas often predicted that Russia would

---

* It may be said that the Greek Church is very tenacious of the Catholic doctrines and Catholic traditions. I answer: The Greek Church cannot continue to have unity of faith, for as all-important controversies on questions of faith have arisen in every age in the past, so all-important questions of a similar kind will arise again ; and, on the other hand, she has no infallible "judex controversiarum"—*i.e.*, no infallible judge of controversies, either in Pope or in General Council—to appeal to, who could settle such matters definitively.

perish by her religious divisions. Now, a Church which is torn by increasing and incurable schisms can hardly have the boldness to pretend that a necessary, unfailing bond of unity is one of her essential characteristics.

But now, which *alone* amongst all the Churches has this mark of unity? Cardinal Wiseman gives the answer. He says there is one simple way of demonstrating which Church has the right to claim it—*i.e.*, by showing which is the Church which *alone actually* claims it. He adds, that if we find that all other Churches give up their right and title to it, it follows that they can have no pretension to it; and if only one Church assumes it as one of its characteristics, assuredly we have enough to prove that it alone possesses it. "With regard to unity," he observes, "all say that they believe in one Church, and profess that the true Church can be only one. But the Catholic Church is the only one which requires absolute unity of faith among all its members; not only so, but—as by principles alone I wish to try the question —the Catholic Church is the only one that holds a principle of faith essentially supposing unity as the most necessary quality of the Church. The Catholic Church lays down, as its principle and ground of faith, that all mankind must believe whatever she decides and sanctions, with the assistance of the Holy Ghost; and this is a principle necessarily directed to bring all men's minds into oneness of thought. Its essence, therefore—its very soul—that which gives it individuality—is the principle of unity.

The principle of the others is, that each individual must judge for himself and make out his own system of faith : now dispersion, dissension, and variety are necessarily the very essence of a Church which adopts that principle. And this, in fact, is practically demonstrated. For Leslie acknowledges that the character, nature, and principle of private judgment is to produce variety and difference of opinion, and even civil and general war. Thus clearly in the Catholic Church alone does the principle of unity exist " (*Lectures on the Catholic Church*, Lect. ix., pp. 317, 318, third edit.).

Yes, the Catholic Church, and the Catholic Church alone, can claim this essential mark of truth, for she alone actually possesses it. Her mode of teaching excludes absolutely every principle, prerogative, or privilege that could lead to contradiction in the domain of doctrine. She interdicts the use of private judgment in matters of faith now—she has ever interdicted it—and she will continue to interdict it to the end of time. Free inquiry, individual preference, liberty of mind, freedom of thought, private judgment, in the domain of faith, are words which she has no ears to hear. She will not, she cannot, listen to them. They would rend the rock on which she rests. She takes her stand on the unchanging truths of Him who built her ; and she will tolerate no human pretensions which would tend to split them asunder. Nor will she suffer any sophistry, however plausible, that would generate the least deviation from them. Her teaching is one, absolute, clear, unerring, emphatic, definitive. No creeds of human origin can rear their heads within her pale, except to be branded with her loud and withering anathemas. She will never recognise any appeal from her tribunal. She will suffer none of her children to sit in judgment upon her decrees. In all places, at all times, in all circumstances, her voice is unchanging. High position, boundless worth, literary attainments, vast erudition, transcendent ability, genius even of the highest order make no difference. With the king and the subject, the philosopher and the savage, the rich and the poor, the young and the old, her method of teaching is the same. To the youth of fifteen and the old man of fourscore she speaks in the same tone. To each generation of her children, as they grow up to an age to understand her symbol of faith, she says with the authoritative voice of her founder: "You are but of yesterday; you are but fifteen, twenty, thirty, fifty, eighty, at most a hundred years of age. *You* did not live in the days of Jesus Christ to hear the doctrines He commanded to be believed, and the precepts He commanded to be fulfilled. But *I* lived in His time, for *I* am His Church, His spouse. And I have brought down in my bosom through the centuries that have since rolled away the doctrines He revealed to the world, and the sense in which He meant them to be received—the precepts He imposed, and the manner in which He meant them to be fulfilled. It is *mine* to teach you. It is *yours* to listen and to believe. But it is *not* yours, and it never *can* be yours, to build up a creed out of your own head."

This mode of teaching bears upon it the impress of Divine institution. Here is a bond of unity. Here is a bulwark of unity. Here is unity in principle and unity in practice—unity in word and unity in meaning. Neither practical error nor speculative error, neither Rationalism, nor Indifferentism, nor Liberalism, nor Latitudinarianism, nor Agnosticism, nor any other religious system of human invention, can ever find a shelter in this impregnable citadel of God's one, perfect, unchanging, everlasting truth.

CHAPTER II.

Universality or Catholicity.

Section I.

THAT Church which Christ founded must have universality or catholicity as one of her essential marks.

What is meant by universality as an essential mark of the one true Church of Christ? It is well to define our meaning, for wrong impressions may easily be formed.

Universality or catholicity,* in the sense in which it is an essential mark of the one true Church, is nothing else but such extension as to time, territorial space, number of members, as will make it clear to all who choose to inquire that she is the only Church amongst all religious bodies in which is found permanent unity of faith springing from a necessary unfailing

---

* Or, as in the words of the Catechism—" The Church is catholic or universal, because she has subsisted in every age, is spread through all nations, and shall last to the end of time" (*Maynooth Catechism*).

principle of faith ; and therefore the only one which can justly claim to be the Church instituted by Christ.

Hence when we hold that she must have universality as an essential note of her truth, we do not mean that she must necessarily exist in every country of the globe, from pole to pole, simultaneously. Neither do we mean that she must have at all times, or at any time, the greater part of the human race enrolled as members of her fold. Neither do we mean that in every period of her history, or in *any* period of it, it must be clear that in point of numbers she is far ahead of the various heretical and schismatical sects taken collectively. Nor do we mean even that her members must necessarily be more numerous than some individual heresy or schism, which, for the hour, has become particularly rampant and particularly popular. No. Numbers however great, space however wide, duration however long—none of these things singly, nor all of them collectively, can constitute universality in the sense in which it is a necessary note of the one true Church. Universality is rather the transparent medium through which her unity becomes strikingly visible. For it is, we may say, the unity of the Church illustrated and manifested in a sufficiently large and wide sphere, to make that unity a visible, striking, unmistakable proof of truth ; since *such* unity, producing oneness of thought on so large a scale, holding permanently so many people of different times, of different climes, different tongues, different character, in one and the same faith, is something which cannot be accounted for on merely natural grounds, and consequently presupposes the Divine institution of the thing to which it belongs.

Hence, that the Church of Christ be universal, in the sense in which universality is a mark of her truth, it is not necessary that she should be simultaneously and mathematically universal. Her action on the nations of the world is not to be measured by mathematical dimensions : majority of numbers and vastness of territory do not constitute this mark.

It is not impossible that God, whose wise Providence rules all things, might allow one nation after another to lose the faith, in punishment of the abuse of grace— might permit persecution so to cripple her power and thin her children that her sphere would be narrowed within a very much smaller space than that which she now occupies. He might allow Liberalism, Agnosticism, Atheism, to wrench from her bosom as many members as she lost in the great apostasy of the sixteenth century, without her acquiring any New World, where millions of conversions would compensate her for her loss. Such diminution of her numbers, however—such narrowing of her sphere, would not deprive her of that universality which is an essential mark of truth. However small the numbers to which apostasy might reduce her—however narrow the limits within which persecution may confine her, there would still shine on her brow the star that would make it clear that she was the Church of all times and of all nations —her identity with the Church of the centuries and generations of the past would be clearly discernible ; and she would continue ever to be the Church, of which alone it could be said, that she, and she only, had the potentiality of universality—that is, a power that would make her even absolutely universal, if the passions, prejudices, and obstinacy of men did not prevent her from doing so.

Now it is on this potentiality, power, or capacity of universality, that I wish chiefly to ground my argument. Although the members of the Church in communion with Rome reach a higher figure than is reached by the members of all other Christian bodies taken collectively, yet I will not take advantage of this majority of numbers. Numbers ebb and flow. The crops of the earth in some particular year may be fourfold what they were the year before, and tenfold what they are the year following. Universal war and widespread epidemic may reduce the population of the earth by many millions in a decade.

No; I will take ground which cannot be disputed; for it is my settled purpose not to draw any inference except from premises which will be easily granted, or which at least can admit of being proved. I will argue from that inborn property or power of universality which is essential to the very existence of the Church of Christ, and of which visible universality is nothing but the external manifestation. This is the point on which I wish to insist most.

Whichever Church is Christ's was His Church before she became actually universal in any sense. She *could* and *did* exist before she was widely spread. She was as truly His Church while she was still confined within the walls of Jerusalem. as when some centuries later she had reduced the East and the West under her sway, and counted her members in millions. But she never *was* His Church, and she never *could* be His Church, without having the innate potentiality of universality. This inherent power of making herself universal, as far as people will allow her to become universal, is essential to her being. It was implanted in her on the day of Pentecost, when she stepped forth in all her completeness from the hands of her Founder, and when His Divine Spirit descended into her to dwell in her for ever. And the vast space she was afterwards to cover, and the millions of members she was afterwards to count in the course of her long and glorious history, were to be but the visible results of that power in action.

I have said : Whichever Church is Christ's must be one which has the potentiality of universality. This statement is easily proved.

As Christ died for all, He instituted His Church for the salvation of all, since He meant His Church to be instrumental in saving all whom He died to redeem. The salvation of the whole human race was the sole object He had in view when He founded her on the everlasting rock, and when He gave His Apostles the great commission to bear her message of faith to all the nations of the earth. And it was that she might be instrumental in saving the human race, not merely in one stage of its career, but in all its generations to the end of time, that He promised to remain with her all days down to the consummation. In other words, He did not bring her into life that she might save the people of Asia only, or of Africa only, or of Europe only, or of Ireland, England, or Scotland only, but that she might save the people of all countries and of all centuries. His intention and desire, in founding her, covered exactly the same space and the same duration as was covered by His intention and desire in working out Redemption. As His Redemption was to take in the people of all places and of all ages, so did He mean His Church to embrace, within her bosom, mankind of every place and of every time. If He redeemed all, it was that all might be saved; if He instituted His Church, it was that all might be saved by her, for through her He meant the fruits of His copious and universal Redemption to be communicated to all for whom He shed His blood and gave His life.

No one can deny that such were His intentions. That some, that many men in every age were to refuse to listen to her voice, to shut their eyes to her signs, to persecute, to imprison, to murder those who sought to bring to them her saving message, does not interfere with His merciful and loving designs. As His blood was to be shed for many in vain—so His Church would be founded for many in vain—both for many within her and for many without her, who would persistently refuse her proffered graces.

Let it be borne in mind that as yet I am not saying which Church has this essential mark of truth. My contention at present is that Christ meant His Church for the salvation of the people of ALL nations and of ALL times.

But if He meant her to save all He must have meant her to REACH all, as far at least as people would allow themselves to be reached by her. In other words, He must have so constructed her that she should have the potentiality or power of making herself even absolutely universal, unless the malice, blindness, obstinacy, passions, or prejudices of men prevented her from doing so. More than this, He must have meant her to be continually striving throughout all time to enlarge her sphere—to make her light shine more and more widely—to bring her gospel of truth to those who had it not. All reasonable Christians will admit that any Church which does not fit in this frame can have no claim to be considered the one true Church of Christ.

Now here, quite independently of any argument taken from comparison of numbers—quite independently of any argument taken from the relative success of the efforts made by the various Christian denominations to convert the heathen—quite independently too of any argument taken from the names of those Churches or sects, whose names indicate their geographical boundaries, and mark them out as national or local institutions;—quite independently of all this, we have ground enough to show that the Church of England has not this essential mark of the one true Church of Christ. *Not only has she not it, she cannot by possibility ever have it.*

Section II.

No Church which has not unity of faith, springing from a necessary, unfailing principle, conservative of that unity, can ever possibly have the potentiality of universality; and, therefore, can never possibly have the mark of universality, since the mark is but the outgrowth of the innate power. As long as it has not a bond to keep it united as one and the same thing, it can never have in itself the germ of universal growth. Its inherent elements of discord will prevent it from mu!tiplying in its original form.

An army, in point of overwhelming numbers, perfect discipline, complete equipment, skill of commander, invincible courage on the part of its officers and of its rank and file, may be, in the opinion of the most competent judges, more than strong enough to subdue all the nations of the earth.

It has hardly begun, however, its work of universal conquest, when discord becomes visible in its ranks. It is split into two opposite camps which fight against each other, and continue to fight against each other. Reconciliation is hopeless. The elements of division spread, and break up the two great sections into minor opposing bands, until every trace of union has disappeared.

It is clear such an army, however numerous, however brave, however well armed and well officered, can never reduce the world under one sceptre: actual division makes that impossible. In like manner, some new religion appears. It panders to men's prejudices, flatters men's passions, professes to impose some semblance of restraint, while it leaves them comparatively free both as to faith and to morals. It is easily made plausible through the ingenious rhetoric of its propagandists—it quickly becomes popular with the multitude—it may make proselytes in thousands in the hour of wild, unreasoning excitement—it may even bring some nations under its sway for the time; but having within itself the elements of division, being devoid of that union which constitutes at once strength and individuality, having no bond of cohesion to keep it together as one united whole, it will be rent inevitably into different sects before it gets half across the world, and so will fail utterly to reduce mankind under one symbol of faith. Hence, no Church which has not an unfailing, necessary principle of unity can ever possibly have the potentiality or mark of universality. Even granting its facilities, which can never be realised in practice, its teaching can never by any possibility spread universally. Remove all impediments, put away all opposition springing from the blindness, obstinacy, malice, passions or prejudices of men, let all the nations of the earth be cheerfully willing to listen to and to embrace its teaching, let every circumstance of time and place favour its apostolate; and withal, it cannot possibly ever have the mark of universality, since it does not possess the inborn power from which universality springs. It will teach one nation one set of doctrines, and another nation their corresponding contradictories; or, perhaps, it will teach one and the same nation a hundred distinctly different creeds.

We have not far to go to find a practical illustration of this. Look at the Church of England, within the very shores from which she takes her name. Can she be said to have kept her members in the same belief even in that very territory within which she is dominant?

Certainly not. In the very realm where the religion she teaches is the established one, where she is helped, subsidised, encouraged, stimulated by the machinery of the greatest civil power the sun ever shone upon, she has not succeeded in keeping her members in the same creed, except in the broad sense of a widespread, universal, multiform, antagonism to the Church of Rome. She may indeed have the mark of universality in that sense. But to say that England ever did profess, or is professing now, Protestantism as one united, uniform creed, would be as great an error as to assert that England, France, Germany, Austria, Russia, Turkey, China, North and South America, were united under one and the same crowned head.

Those who profess her religion at the present moment are not under her control, either as to doctrines of faith or precepts of morality. *She* is entirely under *their* control. They circumscribe her boundaries, define her sphere, mark out her work, sit in judgment upon her, frequently take the punishment of clergymen into their own hands, make decrees for the regulation of her worship, and change them at their pleasure. And as to foreign operations for the propagation of the Gospel, it is only when they furnish her with ample means and promise to hold over her the strong arm of civil protection, that she will make any move to preach her divided creed to the heathen. And then, *just because her creed is a divided one*, her effort is an absolute failure.

To this fact—the fact that *in* her are found the elements of inevitable discord, interminable contradiction, endless division—her notorious want of success in her attempts to evangelise the people of pagan lands is to be ascribed. The average pagan, though not deeply read, though not skilled in close reasoning, has nevertheless sense enough to perceive that there cannot be much truth in a religion in which there are so many opposite opinions. Some of them, after hearing contrary expositions of faith from the lips of those sectarian missionaries who sought to Christianise them, have been heard to say that Christians seemed to have as many different religions as paganism had gods. "There is no greater barrier," says Mr. Colledge, a Protestant British official in China, "to the spread of the Gospel of our Saviour among the heathen than the division and splitting which have taken place among the various orders of Christians themselves. Let us ask any intelligent Chinese what he thinks of this, and he will tell us that these persons cannot be influenced by the same great principle, but that Europe and America must have as many Christs as China has gods."

A Church which has not a bond of unity proceeding from an unfailing principle of unity can never become universal. A thing which has not permanent identity can never possess the power or quality of universal assimilation.

The Church of England has no bond of unity, and therefore can never possibly have that mark or capacity of universality which is essential to the one true Church of Christ.

The Church of Rome, as we have seen, is the only one which possesses such a bond of unity, and hence she alone can ever possibly realise universality in practice. And as a matter of fact, as we shall see later, she alone has ever practically realised it.

Section III.

This potentiality of universality must be one that slumbers not : it must be ever active and energising.

Whichever Church is Christ's must be one of which impartial history can testify, that she has been striving actively and energetically ever from her first beginnings and throughout her whole career to propagate her faith more and more widely through pagan lands. Any Church which has not exhibited at all times, when there was any opportunity of doing so, this characteristic of active zeal for the conversion of the heathen, cannot have any claim to be considered the one true Church of Christ.

If there be any persons who have any difficulty in granting this, a few words will make the matter clear.

The sun cannot be in the heavens above us without sending forth rays of light. There may be an eclipse, there may be a mist black as night, still, from the very fact that he is in the sky, he must send forth his beams, and those beams must reach us, unless some accidental cause darkens the medium through which they are meant to be conveyed to us.

The Church was designed by Christ, her Founder, to be the light of the world, and to be the light of the world of every century and of every generation.

He Himself who is the Eternal Sun of Justice and who styled Himself the Light of the World, promised to be in her all days, that she might be such. He meant her light to shine upon the people of all times and of all places. Consequently, His desire to dispel the darkness of paganism did not end with the death of His first Apostles. When He gave them the commission to teach all nations, He foresaw that the martyr's death would overtake them before they had succeeded in making His Gospel known to all nations. He could not mean that as soon as the grave had closed over their remains, His Church was to cease entirely the work of propagating the faith, and was thenceforward to make no further effort to make her light shine in those regions which were still in the darkness of idolatry and in the shadow of death. We cannot hold that such was His design without being forced to the conclusion that, while He had at heart the salvation of those who lived in the days of His first Apostles, He had no concern as to what became of the pagan nations of the second, third, and fourth centuries, and of every century to the end of time.

It is clear He meant her to continue throughout all ages her efforts to evangelise the nations—to spread her light farther and farther over the earth ; else she would fail to fulfil the end for which He founded her.

It is clear also that if He promised to be with His first Apostles by a special presence of His power and guidance, in order to stimulate and help them to do the work of propagating His faith everywhere, He meant that promised presence to extend to their successors throughout all generations; for the simple reason, that the dissipation of the darkness of idolatry, and the replacing it by the light of His Gospel, were works which would be as dear to His Sacred Heart throughout all time, as they were on the memorable day when He spoke the words—" Going, teach all nations ".

Since, then, Christ dwells permanently in His Church—since He is the light of the world, since He must have at all times a constant, active, efficacious desire that His light should illuminate the whole earth, it follows that His Church must be one, of which the unprejudiced historian can relate that, during her whole career, she, above all others, has manifested a strong impulse—a necessarily active desire to bring heathen nations within her communion.

But which amongst all the Churches now existing can honestly claim from the impartial records of the past this glorious testimony?

Can the Anglican Church, the Lutheran Church, or the Calvinistic Church lay any claim thereto? No. They did not begin to exist till towards the middle of the sixteenth century, and consequently could not have evangelised the peoples of the long centuries that had passed away before they were born. And even for the few years of their comparatively short career, they cannot stand the application of this test. For they had been a considerable period in existence before they showed any inclination at all to make the light of their creed shine on the idolater.

Besides, this was not their scope. Their sphere

was meant to be purely local. Their original framing excluded all idea of organisation for wide foreign missionary enterprise—in fact, for missionary enterprise of any kind. They were to be but a phase of the state in which they were to subsist. They were to be under State-control, and consequently were to partake of the nature of the constitution whose established religion they were to be. And a religion formed to suit the taste of some particular nation is not likely ever to become a religion of universal adoption. A religion that suits the government of one country may not suit the government of another country, and is certain not to suit the government of every country. At all events, being created and kept in life by an act of Parliament, they could not make any move to convert the heathen, unless directed, encouraged, helped, subsidised by the State whose dominant religion they represented. And surely we cannot say that Christ ever meant His Church, which He founded to evangelise all the nations of the earth, to be directed in the measure and exercise of her zeal for the salvation of souls, by the laws of any particular country, and to be guided in her efforts for the propagation of the faith in pagan lands, according to the dictates of any particular civil power.

That I am not making groundless statements, or putting the thing in a false light, will be evident from the following testimonies, which undoubtedly cannot be said to be taken from prejudiced sources.

Lord Macaulay, whose opposition to the Catholic Church is sufficiently known to make it certain that he does not say anything in her praise except what he believes to be true, draws a contrast between her action and that of the Reformed Churches in the seventeenth and eighteenth centuries. In any case, the truth of his statement is patent to all.

He says : " As the Catholics in zeal and union had a great advantage over the Protestants, so had they an infinitely superior organisation. In truth, Protestantism, for aggressive purposes, had no organisation at all. The Reformed Churches were mere national Churches. The Church of England existed for England alone. It was an institution as purely local as the Court of Common Pleas, and was utterly without machinery for foreign operations. The Church of Scotland, in like manner, existed for Scotland alone. The operations of the Catholic Church took in the whole world" (Essay on Ranke's *History of Popery*).

A prominent Presbyterian clergyman speaks in a similar tone in his review of Marshall's well-known volumes entitled *Christian Missions*. He even philosophises on the matter. " During the sixteenth and seventeenth centuries," he says, "the Romish Church girdled the globe with her missions, planting the cross from beyond the wall of China to the Peruvian Cordilleras. Nor is it to be denied that her missionaries, in those years, were men abounding in Christian heroism and sacrifices. Of monetary means she had not so much as any one of our Protestant societies. But she had what, alas ! we so often fail to get—abundance of large-hearted men, ready to do and suffer everything for the faith." He continues :

"This interesting inquiry" (he means the singular success of Catholic missions as contrasted with the evident failure of Protestant missions) "is one which calls for deeper thought and greater fairness than polemical divines have yet allowed it; for the student of history will not be satisfied without some theory or law adequate to account for the undeniable fact, that hitherto the progress of Christianity among the heathen has been carried on chiefly by Romanism, and only in a slight manner as yet by a consistent and scriptural Protestantism" (*North British Review*, May, 1864).

In a very slight manner, indeed, if we look to the results; on a gigantic scale, however, if we consider the enormous sums of money that have been expended by Protestant missionary societies, and the millions of Bibles that have been exported from England and America.

The feeble and fruitless efforts (though numerous) which the Protestant Church of late years has made, do not tend to strengthen her claim to the note of universality.

However, during the last sixty or seventy years, that Church, particularly in England and America, has had an organisation for carrying on missions in pagan lands; and if we are to look to the number of its agents and the magnitude of its resources, a great organisation it has been.

Its emissaries, says Marshall in his *Christian Missions*, are reckoned by thousands and its revenues by millions. "A single English society," we are told, "consumes, in its home expenditure alone, about forty thousand pounds annually, before one native is converted, or even sees a missionary. That is to say, nearly one-fourth of the whole income of a society, maintained for the purpose of spreading the light of the Gospel in heathen countries, is spent in England before one preacher has embarked on his mission" (vol. i., p. 3). It is stated that during the present century, England and America alone, omitting Germany, Switzerland, and all Protestant States of modern Europe, had before the year 1862 expended in the work of missions, including the distribution of Bibles and tracts, at least forty millions sterling.

Do these facts give to Protestantism any claim to that universality which is a mark of the true Church? Do they go any way towards proving that the Protestant Church is identical with the one in which there must be an ever-active impulse, an ever-efficacious zeal to evangelise heathen nations? We shall show, and show it on Protestant testimony, that they prove exactly the contrary.

It is unfortunate for the claims of the Protestant Church that she ever attempted to give missions at all in pagan countries. It is a kind of work for which she was never intended, and which, from her very structure, was quite unnatural to her.

Although the enormous sums of money, contributed to swell her foreign missionary funds, bespeak the generous liberality of many of her religious-minded children, yet the spirit of the missionaries she has sent out, the way in which they have done their work, and the slender results which that work has produced, can only tend, in the mind of all impartial observers, to remove from her farther and farther all resemblance to the Church which was destined to teach all nations through all time, and to be for ever the light of the world.

The signal failure of her missionary efforts in all parts of the world (a failure confessed to by members of her own denomination) makes it clear to evidence that she cannot be that Divine everlasting institution to which was addressed the world-wide commission: " Going, teach all nations ". With all her unlimited resources and all her vast expenditure, she has made but few converts ; and those few, say the same Protestant witnesses, have in most cases been distinguished by becoming worse after their conversion than they were before, and much worse than their heathen compatriots.

While another Church, with hardly any earthly resources—without help from the hand of any civil power—without human appliances of any kind—with nothing except fearless apostolic courage and burning zeal, has, during the same years and in the very same spheres of labour, made converts in multitudes, and has lifted them up from the lowest depths of pagan degradation to a life of practical virtue which has made them an object of wonder to all who have witnessed the change.

That I am not going out of the region of facts, or making unwarrantable statements, will be evident from testimonies I now adduce—all of which are given by

Protestants or by members of various non-Catholic denominations. They are found in Marshall's book on *Christian Missions*, vol. i., from page 9 to 15, with abundant references.

China.

"The attempts of Protestant bodies to evangelise China," says Mr. Antony Grant, author of the *Bampton Lectures* for 1843, "have signally failed."

"Whoever asserts," added Mr. Wingrove Cooke in 1858, "that the Protestant missionaries are making sincere Chinese Christians, must be either governed by delusion or guilty of fraud."

India.

Sir James Brooke, in 1858, speaking before a meeting of the Society for the Propagation of the Gospel, said :—"You have made no progress at all either with the Hindoo or the Mahometan : you are just where you were the very first day that you went to India".

Mr. Clarkson, himself a missionary, speaks in the same tone :—"Every gate," he says, "seems to have been shut, every channel dammed up, by which Gospel streams might force their way".

Mr. Irving goes further still, when speaking of the nominal converts. He says, and says it in accord with a hundred Anglo-Indian witnesses, that "their lax morality shocks the feelings of even their heathen fellow-countrymen",

Ceylon.

The Rev. W. Haward, a Wesleyan missionary, says:
—" The greater part of the Singhalese, whom I designate nominal Christians of the Reformed Religion, are
little more than Christians by baptism ".

" Disappointment was felt in nearly every depart-
ment of the mission," says Dr. Brown in 1854.

" All accounts agree in reporting unfavourably," adds
the Rev. Mr. Tupper in 1856.

Mr. Pridham goes farther.   He deplores in energetic
language that Christianity has made but " leeway ".

Antipodes.

Of Australia, Dr. Lang reported in 1852 :—" There
is no well-authenticated case of the conversion of a
black native to Christianity ".

Mr. Minturn added in 1858 :—" All missionary
efforts among them failed ".

New Zealand.

Mr. Fox declared in 1851 :—" With most of the
natives Christianity is a mere name, entirely inopera-
tive in practice ".

In 1859 Dr. Thomson still repeats that it is only a
rude mixture of paganism and the cross.

Mr. Wakefield, who is confirmed by a multitude of
witnesses, adds the gloomy statement that the converted natives are distinctly inferior in point of moral
character to the unconverted heathen.

Another Protestant authority attests the Colonial verdict, that they are, generally speaking, distinguished from the unconverted as rogues, thieves, and liars.

Oceannica.

Of the Society Islands, a writer in the *Asiatic Journal* reported as long ago as 1832 that " the presence of the missionaries has been productive of more mischief than good ".

Mr. Pridham announced seventeen years later that they had only added a new plague to the evils which they had come to cure.

The Rev. Mr. Hines, Mr. Herman Melville, Commodore Wilkes, Chaplain Laplace, all speak in the same tone.

Africa.

In Western Africa Mr. Tracy reckons eighteen Protestant missionary attempts, without counting Sierra Leone and Goree, all of which failed.

Mr. Duncan candidly declares of those in Dahomey, that the education given by the missionaries is only the means of enabling them to become more perfect in villainy.

Of the Kaffirs in South Africa, Major Dundas reported in 1835 to the House of Commons :—" I believe the missionaries have hardly Christianised a single individual ".

Twenty-three years later, the Rev. Mr. Calderwood declared once more :—" The Kaffirs may be said to have refused the Gospel ".

In North and East Africa it is not even alleged that any converts have been made.

The Levant, Syria and Armenia.

Of the missionaries in the Levant, Sir Adolphus Slade says in 1854, after many years of personal observation :—" Their utter unprofitableness cannot be sufficiently pointed out ".

Of those in Greece, Dr. Hawes reports, they " have felt themselves obliged for the present to withdraw, in a great measure, from the field "—which means, as we shall see, that they were expelled by the people.

Of Jerusalem, Lord Castlereagh tells us :—" The Bishop has scarcely a congregation besides his chaplains, his doctor, and their families ".

Dr. Southgate, an American Protestant Bishop, candidly admits that the only Protestant converts, throughout Turkey and the Levant, " are infidels and radicals who deserve no sympathy from the Christian public ".

And Dr. Wagner declares, after careful examination, that the expensive establishments in Armenia have made no converts.

America.

Finally, the learned author of *The Natural History of Man* warns his readers not to venture upon any comparison between the success of missions to the aboriginal races of North and South America, because their history reveals a contrast so portentous that, as he frankly admits, it must be allowed to cast a deep shade upon the history of Protestantism.

If, then, it is clear that the Protestant Church, before she began to give missions to the heathen, could not possibly have either the mark or the capacity of universality, that fact has become clearer now that she has made the attempt. Indeed we might say that if there were nothing else to prove that she is not the Church of Christ, her uniform want of success in her foreign missionary efforts would be quite enough to prove it. The heathen nations, even on Protestant testimony, have everywhere rejected her teaching; and the few individuals, who pretend to become her disciples, have, on the same testimony, been lower in the scale of morality than they were before their apparent conversion.

Such then is her history. For about two centuries and a half—that is, from her institution till the beginning of this century—she confined her zeal within those dominions to which she owes her creation and to which she owes the continuance of her life. During the whole of that long period she manifested no compassion—no consideration for the poor idolater. She let him go his way, and left him to perish helplessly in his darkness, without making any attempt to stretch out to him the hand of relief, although the constantly increasing commerce of the great empire which she represented gave her every facility for doing so. She remained satisfied with her work at home, enjoyed her repose with dignity, and went on sleeping the sleep of undisturbed peace. Then suddenly, in the beginning of this century (about the year 1805), she awoke from her slumber; shook off her drowsiness, became alive to a sense of her culpable apathy, and seemed anxious to make a great, a vigorous, a stupendous effort for the propagation of the faith—such an effort as would make amends for long and grave neglect. Enormous sums of money for evangelising purposes were produced; missionaries were sent out in thousands to pagan lands; millions of Bibles and numberless tracts were distributed in pagan towns—that is, in pagan ports and all along the coasts. Those publications were sown broadcast, as the farmer sows his grain. They never took root however. The soil proved most ungrateful. And what has been the result? To-day her hands are as empty of fruit as if she had never advanced a step in the direction of foreign missionary enterprise, or as if the idolater had never seen a single leaf of a Bible or tract in his life.

It is evident, then, that neither past nor contemporary history can bear testimony that she has been throughout her career the evangelising Church of the nations.

But now comes the question: Can the Greek schismatical Churches claim this testimony? No. They have never pretended or professed to be missionary Churches at all. They are mere national Churches—purely local institutions like the Church of England: but, *unlike* the Church of England, they have made no attempt even in this nineteenth century to convert the heathen.

As to the Greek-Russian Church, Marshall, speak-ing of it, says :—" It not only fails to convert the heathen tribes subject to the empire, but does not always even wish to do so. It suits," they say, " the secular policy of the Czar to leave them to their idols." " The clergy of Russia, as Tourgeneff, Haxthausen, and others relate, have no disposition for such labours : the State, as Theiner, Dr. Moritz Wagner, and many more have shown, forbids others to supply the defect. Every Catholic priest, says Dr. Wagner, who attempts to convert an idolater is threatened with transportation to Siberia " (*Christian Missions*, vol. i., p. 1).

Hence the Greek schismatical Churches do not and cannot ask to claim from history the testimony, that they have been striving assiduously, throughout their course, to make the light of Christianity shine in heathen lands.

One Church, and one Church alone, can claim this glorious testimony.

Need I say it is the Church of Rome ?

She has been the great evangelist of the nations throughout all time since the days of the Apostles ; and, as we shall see presently, she is the only suc-cessful evangelising Church of the present genera-tion.

As to the past, we need not dwell long in claiming for her a glory which even her bitterest enemies do not attempt to withhold from her. If it be asked, who gave to England that Christianity whose form was changed and mutilated at the Reformation, Venerable Bede answers the question to the satisfaction of all.

Speaking of England's conversion, he says :—" And whereas he (Pope Gregory) bore the pontifical power all over the world, and was placed over the Churches already reduced to the faith, he made our nation, till then given up to idols, the Church of Christ".

Who gave to Germany the religion which she abolished in the revolt of Luther? Do not all impartial records show it came from missionaries who had with them the approval, the credentials, and the blessing of the Roman Pontiff?

Dr. Milman, some years ago Dean of St. Paul's, in his *History of Latin Christianity*, after showing that one nation after another received the Gospel through the voice of the Church of Rome, adds :—" All these conquests of Christianity were in a certain sense the conquests of the Roman See. . . . Reverence for Rome penetrated with the Gospel to the remotest parts. Germany was converted to Latin Christianity. Rome was the source, the centre, the regulating authority recognised by the English apostles to the Teutons. The clergy were constantly visiting Rome as the religious capital of the world . . . and bishops from the remotest parts of the empire, and of regions never penetrated by the Roman arms, looked to Rome as the parent of their faith—if not to an infallible authority, at least to the highest authority in Christendom."

Colonel Mitchell, in his *Life of Wallenstein*, says :— " Deep and indelible is the debt which religion and civilisation owe to the early Roman Pontiffs and to the Church of Rome. They strove long and nobly to forward the cause of human improvement, and it is difficult to say what other power could have exercised so beneficial an influence over the fierce and fiery nations which established themselves on the ruins of the Roman empire, after rooting out all that remained of ancient art and ancient knowledge. Nor were their efforts confined within those territorial limits. Monks and missionaries, disregarding personal danger, penetrated into the forests of Germany and into the distant regions of the North, and, unappalled by the deaths of torture to which so many holy men had fallen victims, preached to the heathen and barbarian the mild doctrines of Christianity, which only sprung up in Europe watered by the blood of saints and martyrs. Even the efforts of the Church to interpose its spiritual power in the direction of temporal matters, and to control the conduct of kings and princes, were beneficial in an age when the clergy alone possessed whatever learning was extant; and the uniformity of belief which rendered all the Western Churches dependent on the Pope, an authority so greatly enlightened, when contrasted with the general darkness of the times, became a principal cause of the progress and prosperity of the Catholic world."

Such the testimonies of Protestant writers.

Who brought the light of the faith to France, and made her a Catholic nation ?—Missionaries who came in the name, and with the authority and benediction, of the See of Rome.

Who evangelised Spain ? Who brought to Austria and her tributaries the faith she now professes ? Who led Ireland and Scotland to a knowledge of the true Gospel? Who gave to the various nations of the East that religion (I mean orthodox religion) which they professed in all its completeness and integrity, till schism rent them from the parent stock?—Either the first Apostles who recognised Peter as their head, or their successors who recognised Peter's See—the See of Rome—as the head of all the Churches, and proclaimed union with that See to be a necessary qualification for membership in the one true fold of Christ.

Go through all the countries of Europe, of Asia, of Africa, that ever professed the Christian religion in its completeness and perfectness, trace their Christianity to its source, and you will find that source to be none other than the energising power—the necessarily active, unfailing impulse to evangelise—which is ever found in the Church of which Peter's successor is the visible head.

All impartial records of the past agree in stating the undeniable fact, that, from the days of the Apostles down to the present time, the Church of Rome has been constantly, untiringly exerting her power to bring idolatrous nations under the sway of the Gospel of Christ. There is no other Church of which this can be said. She alone, amongst all the religious bodies which now exist, has manifested throughout her career that sacred energy—that holy, earnest, necessarily active zeal for the conversion of the heathen and the heretic which must ever characterise the Church in which dwells the Saviour of souls, who founded her as much for the salvation of the people of the nine-teenth century, and of every century to the day of doom, as for the salvation of the people who lived in the age which witnessed her institution.

Now let us place her side by side with those sects which have in this century affected to surpass her in zeal for the propagation of the faith, and have tried to wrench from her her title of Universal Teacher. Have they succeeded ?—No. They cannot dispute her ex-clusive claim to that title for the pre-Reformation period ; nor can they dispute that she alone was the apostle of pagan countries during the seventeenth and eighteenth centuries. During those two centuries, while Protestantism in England and on the Conti-nent was being divided into endless sects, which were battling with one another continually—while their respective leaders were excommunicating each other with implacable acrimony, the Church of Rome, as Dr. Hanna observes, was girdling the globe with her missions. While no schismatical or heretical herald of the Gospel had, as yet, set out from Europe for any barbarous land, *her* apostles were already preaching " in labour and painfulness, in many watchings, in hunger and thirst, in many fastings," and were reaping an abundant harvest in China, Japan, India, Africa, Paraguay—everywhere. This our opponents cannot deny.

Till the eighteenth century, then, she continued to be the sole Teacher of heathendom. Has she lost her claim to that title in this the nineteenth century? Have her rivals uncrowned her ? Have the sects supplanted her? Have *they* done any work of zeal in heathen lands which *she* has not done on a larger scale and immeasurably better? Has the character of *their* zeal transcended *hers*? Have *they* gone far away from the larger centres of population, penetrated into the outlying and remote districts of the savages, and shown themselves unselfish in enduring hunger, thirst, and cold and heat; while *hers* have enjoyed a dignified repose in some comfortable dwelling situated in an eligible quarter of the large city? Have *they* in times of persecution shed their blood profusely, and given up their lives generously and courageously; while *hers*, like cowards, ran away at the first appearance of danger? Have *they* done more for the education of the savage hordes than *she* has done? Have they produced more abundant fruits? Have they made more converts? And have *their* converts been remarkable for practical faith, firmness in trial, intense fervour, earnest devotion, heroic constancy; while *hers* have been distinguished by their coldness, carelessness, apathy, fickleness, gross immorality?

Impartial witnesses shall give the answer, and their answer will show that, while for eighteen hundred years the Church of Rome *alone* possessed, and *alone* could claim, the title of Church of the Universe—yet never has that title shone out so conspicuously, appeared in such striking light, as in the present century, in which the sects have worked by her side in the same fields of labour, and, in spite of all the help human resources could give, have failed utterly everywhere; whereas SHE has prospered to a degree which can only be explained by help from on high, by special aid from the hand of Him whose blessing is with those whom He Himself has chosen, and *not* with those who have tried to intrude themselves into His fold.

It is a common saying that things look brighter by contrast. Never has there been a contrast more striking than that presented by the marvellous fruits which have followed the efforts made by the missionaries of the Catholic Church when compared with the uniform barrenness which has ever attended the labours of their antagonists. It looks, says Mr. Marshall, as if Almighty God, in His wise Providence, meant to take all controversy between the Church and the sects entirely out of *human* hands into His *own*, and to decide the matter Himself by applying His own Supreme test—" By their fruits you shall know them ".

Here are accounts from Protestant sources—at all events, non-Catholic sources :—

China.—" The number of conversions effected by Protestants," says Mr. Hausmann, who dedicates his book to Mr. Guizot, and seems to profess an equal indifference to all sorts of religion, " is perfectly insignificant when compared with those effected by Catholics."

" The religion of Catholics," says Baron Von Haxthausen, " extends itself more and more in the north of the empire ; and even in Pekin itself their number is said to exceed forty thousand."

Mr. Montgomery Martin, a warm-hearted opponent

of the Catholic religion, observes :—" Perhaps there are not more than twenty or thirty Christian Chinese, while Catholicism numbers its tens and hundreds of thousands ".

" It is superfluous," writes Mr. Osmund Tiffany, with reference to his Protestant companions, " to say aught of missionary labours, simply because these have little or no importance."

" Great progress has been silently made," says Sir Oscar Oliphant, in 1857 (though he does not so much as allude to the Protestant attempts), " and continues to be made."

" There is something inexplicable," says the Rev. Howard Malcolm, " in the sterility of the Protestant missions ; for the Catholic missionaries, with very limited resources, have made a great many proselytes, their worship has become popular, and everywhere excites the attention of the public."

" Little has been done," says another, " by missionaries in China except printing books."

" The Protestants," observes Mr. Leitch Ritchie, " have as yet confined their efforts to the distribution of books along the sea-coast ; the result not being in the meantime of any obvious importance."

" We have no proof," adds a candid American missionary, " that the thousands of books thrown among the people have converted a single individual."

" The activity of the missionaries of the Romish Church in China," says Sir John Davis, " has no rival as to numbers or enterprise."

" For many a long, toilsome year," says the Secretary

of a London Missionary Society, in 1855, "has the
Christian missionary been labouring for this people
. . . unblessed with the knowledge of any successful
issues of his labour" (Marshall, *Christian Missions*,
vol. i., chap. ii., pp. 286-8).

Mr. Marshall, alluding to the praise given by Protestant testimony to the zeal of Catholic missions,
says :—"During half a century Protestant writers,
filled with the same involuntary admiration which the
pagans had often manifested with greater energy, have
not ceased to celebrate the courage, devotion, and
charity of the Catholic missionaries in China.   From
Ricci to the latest martyr who gained his crown only
yesterday, they have recognised, without understanding, the same tokens of a supernatural calling.   Even
Morrison was constantly comparing them with himself,
though apparently without deriving instruction from
the contrast."

Speaking of the Catholic missionary, Morrison
says :—" He is willing to sacrifice himself : he offers
himself up to God ".

" They will be equalled by few and rarely excelled
by any," is the joint confession of Mr. Milne and Mr.
Medhurst, " for they spared not their lives unto death,
but overcame by the blood of the Lamb."

" That they were holy and devoted men," says Mr.
Malcolm, " is proved by their pure lives and serene
martyrdom."

" They appear to me," observes Mr. Power, " to
surpass any men I ever met with, they were so forget-
ful of self, so full of pity and compassion for others."

" Their self-denying hard labour is truly wonderful," says Mr. D'Ewes.

" It is a pity that all missionaries are not equally self-sacrificing," adds Mr. Scarth.

" We cannot refuse them our respect," says Colonel Mountain.

" They regard neither difficulties nor discouragements," writes Mr. Sirr.

" I cannot refrain," exclaims Mr. Robertson, " from admiring the heroism, the devotedness, and superiority of the Catholic missionaries."

" On the other hand," continues Mr. Marshall, " the same impartial witnesses who had seen them at their work speak only with sorrow and disgust of the Protestant missionaries in China, in spite of active sympathy with their religious opinions.* Morrison, they tell us, never ventured out of his house, preached only with the doors securely locked, gave books with such precaution that it could not be traced to him, and only ventured on operations which were not of a dazzling or heroic order. Milne found preaching the Gospel in China difficult and ran away. Gulzlaff made his fortune, and then ceased to call himself a missionary. Medhurst could only repeat : ' Why are we not successful in conversions?' Tomlin abandoned the work to the Pope, Mahomet, and Brahma.

* I am aware that some unselfish and generous-hearted clergy-men of non-Catholic denominations have gone on a mission of zeal to foreign lands to try to convert the heathen. The testi-monies, however, which I have cited, and cited entirely from NON-CATHOLIC SOURCES, refer to the great bulk of Sectarian missionaries.

Smith was content to revile the men whom he dared not imitate, to fling Bibles on dry banks, and to provoke the scornful rebukes of his own flock. The rest listened to far-off tidings of what was happening in the interior; or drank wine and played cards on Sunday; or refused to visit the sick in the hospitals; or accepted a skulking and precarious sojourn in obscurity and disguise."

Such is the Protestant account of them.

"They surround themselves with comforts," says Mr. Power, "squabble for the best house, higgle for wares, and provoke contempt by a lazy life."

"We are grieved to the heart's core," writes Mr. Sirr, "to see so many of the Protestant missionaries occupy their time in secular pursuits, trading and trafficking."

Mr. Marshall continues: "The converts, as we have seen, of whom a million belong to the Church, and five, by a sanguine estimate, to the sects, display the same difference of character as their teachers. What the Catholic Chinese were, from the sixteenth to the nineteenth century, we know: what they have been since 1805, hostile witnesses have told us. In spite of torments, never exceeded in duration and intensity, more than half a million have been added to the Church since Timkowski visited Pekin and found that many thousand persons had embraced Christianity, even among the members of the Imperial family; and that the President of the Criminal Tribunal in that city was obliged to relax his severity, because nearly all his relations and servants were Christians. And so exactly have these Chinese neophytes, in every province of the empire, resembled the primitive disciples, that even the Mandarins have been forced to confess from their judgment-seats, in presence of so much virtue and heroism : ' Truly this Christian religion is a good religion '."

Mr. Marshall proceeds : " The rare Protestant converts, on the other hand, the scum of a Chinese seaport, dishonest pensioners of an immoral bounty, who at one time run off with the communion plate, at another with cases of type or whatever else they can lay their hands upon, have been everywhere of such a class that, in the words of a candid witness, anxiety to obtain them has been converted into anxiety about those who were obtained.   And even the teachers and catechists employed by English or American missionaries, brutalised by opium and quite as willing, as Dr. Berncastle says, to teach Buddhism as Anglicanism or Methodism, for the same wages, only accept Protestant baptism as a condition of their employment, and appreciate it so warmly that their whole care thenceforth is to prevent others from sharing the baptism with them, lest they should share the wages also" (Marshall, *Christian Missions*, vol. iii., pp. 409-14).

Let the impartial Christian look these facts in the face : let him view them in the light of faith : let him ponder on them with unbiassed mind, and he will have no difficulty in deciding which class of missionaries has the stronger claim to be considered the apostles of the Church, which was destined in the designs of the Most High to be the Teacher of the nations. If he looks at the Catholic missionary and the Sectarian missionary in the field of labour, if he observes the character of their zeal, their daily life, their domestic relations, their method of work, their surroundings, the difference of their condition as to human help and national patronage, their different attitude in the face of danger ; if he will only weigh all this seriously, then, quite independently of the relative results of their labours alluded to above, he will find it easy to answer to himself the following questions :—

Which Church is making those efforts to convert the heathen, which an unprejudiced conscience will say look most like the efforts that ought to be made by a Church in which the Redeemer of the world is ever dwelling ?

Whose work in spreading the faith has most appearance of the impress of the Holy Ghost upon it ?

Which Church can, with most show of reason, claim to be the one which is still fulfilling the great commission—" Teach all nations "? Is it the one which, not merely throughout all the past, but even in the present generation, can count numbers of heroic men who have shed their blood and given away their lives in their glorious efforts to evangelise the pagan world ? Or is it one which neither at the present time nor at any time in a history of three hundred years can hardly point to an individual who died the martyr's death or risked life in the most distant way, in proof of the earnestness of a desire to bring the blessings of Christianity to the home of the idolater?

Which of the two missionaries is the more likely to win to Christ the idolaters of China or the Indians of America? Is it the man who, at the expense of all earthly comforts, at the risk of health, and even of life, searches them out in their native forests and mountains, who lives on the same fare, lodges in their cabins, observes their manners and customs, who trains them in the habits of industry, cleanliness, self-respect, who instructs and preaches to them in their remotest wildernesses, who prays with them, sympathises with them, shares their joys and sorrows, uses every available means to humanise, civilise, and Christianise them? Or is it the man who seldom, if ever, goes beyond the walls of the city, where waves the flag of the nation whose national Church he represents, and who, if he *does* make an advance into some outlying district, will not move an inch except as far as there are guns and bayonets to protect him?

Which of the two missionaries reflects more perfectly the Apostle of Christ? Is it the missionary who, having vowed perpetual chastity, free from all domestic ties, untrammelled by earthly obligations of any kind, detached from all the goods of life, leaving behind him the friends nearest and dearest to his heart, sets out gaily and joyfully to bear the light of the Gospel to the heathen? Or is it the married missionary whose slow movements are made slower still by the encumbrance of a wife and family? Is it likely that the man who is thus hampered by matrimonial and family ties will have any inclination to risk his life in propagating the Gospel, while he shrinks from making his wife a widow and his children orphans? Will *he* care to leave his comfortable home in the large city and to spend months and years catechising and instructing the heathens of the interior in their remote and savage solitudes? No. Such sacrifices need not be expected. His desire to multiply the members of Christ's fold, and to bring the light of the Gospel to the savage tribes of heathendom, is sure to yield to his attachment to domestic happiness, to wife, to children, and, above all, to anxiety for the safety of his own life.

The efforts of missionaries of this kind are not likely to prove successful in extending the sway of the Gospel in those regions which are outside the pale of Christianity. Heathen populations will never be converted by the mere distribution of Bibles and tracts. The thing has been tried, and tried on a gigantic scale, for over seventy years, and has resulted not merely in hopeless failure, but in having the Scriptures profaned wherever this indiscriminate scattering has taken place. It is well known, that those huge piles of Bibles which are exported from England and America scarcely ever get beyond the city to whose harbour they are shipped. It is well known, too, that in the city itself which has the privilege of receiving such cargo the profane uses to which they are applied by the pagans, for whose conversion they were intended, have shocked the men who had to perform the ungrateful task of superintending their distribution. Wadding for guns, parcel-paper for tea, sugar, and other groceries, are some of the many disrespectful purposes to which these publications are devoted by the very people for whose enlightenment they were translated, printed, exported, and scattered through the large towns and along the sea-coast. Besides, the great bulk of the population for which they are meant never see them. The savages in the mountains and forests, and in the villages far away in the interior, are not aware of the liberal distribution which takes place in the large cities and along the seaboard. And even if they *were* aware of it, it is not probable they would travel so far to get a book of which they have never heard a word and cannot know the value. And the zeal of those whose ostensible duty it is to enlighten the savage hordes never leads them to encounter danger by travelling a thousand miles into the remote districts for the purpose of distributing those copies of the Written Word personally.

More than this, a large proportion of the persons who are fortunate enough to receive a copy of the Bible cannot read, and of those who can read, not one in a thousand can understand the meaning. There is no preaching accompaniment to supply explanation. The preaching is often carried on in the presence of a few individuals, and with locked doors. The tracts, which are meant to be a key to the Inspired Word, are applied to ignominious purposes similar to those to which the Bible itself is devoted. But even if they were applied to the uses for which they are designed by their distributors, they would not produce the desired effect, since in most cases they are more obscure than the thing they propose to elucidate.

Now, if the faith is to come by hearing, pagan populations will never have it through teaching of this kind. When Bibles and tracts are thrown upon them in showers, and left to be picked up or to remain on the ground at random, what can be expected? Is the speedy conversion of multitudes of savages likely to be the result? Can we picture to ourselves Peter, John, Paul, and the other Apostles striving to convert the Gentiles by any such process? We do not read that the Apostles distributed any writings at all. And if these first heralds of the faith appeared on earth now, could we imagine them living a life of ease and indolence in a comfortable, well-furnished residence in the large city, and contenting themselves with sowing broadcast copies of the Scriptures and explanatory tracts, and with doing this only in places where they could afford to do it without any risk of health or of life?

Had they or their successors followed such a method no pagan nation would ever have been converted to the faith. And what is more, had Christ meant this to be the way in which heathen tribes were to be won to His Gospel, He surely would have arranged in His wise providence that the art of printing should be discovered thirteen hundred years earlier; or, at all events, that at least half of those who became members of

His Church should have hardly any occupation throughout life except that of transcribing Bibles and tracts for the conversion of those who were still in the darkness of idolatry.

Hence, I repeat, that if there were nothing else to prove that the sects have nothing in common, either singly or collectively, with the universal Church of Christ, their method of propagating the Gospel among the heathen and their total failure everywhere would be abundantly sufficient. To be convinced that such a method was inadequate to the end to be attained, it was not necessary to know the consequent universal failure. Any observer, of even ordinary penetration, would have pronounced such failure a foregone conclusion. The effort, however, which they have made —and made on such a gigantic scale, and under such favourable circumstances, with millions of money at their command, and all the resources of human influence, and all the help great civil power could give —has only served to bring out into stronger relief the truth that the mere " wide " circulation of Bibles and tracts can never bring a heathen population under the sway of Christianity.

But apart fron this, even if the sects had found the pagans cheerfully willing to accept their Bibles and to accept their creed, and had converted them and received them in their respective folds, they would not have advanced one iota towards establishing a claim to the mark of universality. For, in such a supposition, they would have formed them, *not* into one universal, undivided Church, but into as many

Churches as equalled the number of opposite religions which they themselves represented,—and that number was legion.

Sectarian missionaries may preach to the heathen, and may distribute Bibles in millions to them " every year," to the day of doom, and withal, their divided creed can never possibly become universal,—for the simple reason, that *it is a* divided creed. A Church which has no bond of unity can never multiply in its original form, and therefore can never have the note of universality. A thing which has no permanent identity can never possess the quality of universal assimilation.

I have said that never did the claim of the Catholic Church to be the sole authorised evangelist of the nations appear in clearer light than in this century, which has seen the contrast in heathen lands between *her* missions and those given by her rivals. The thousands, and tens of thousands, of conversions which she has wrought in China, in North and South America, in Africa, and elsewhere, have proclaimed her to be the Mother of unfailing fruitfulness ; while the sects have been stricken everywhere with perpetual sterility.

But the title of " Catholic," or " Church of the World," has been vindicated nearer home, and not long ago. It has been the privilege of this generation to witness the most striking manifestation of her universality that the world has ever seen. Nothing else could have shown so clearly that only the limits of the world can bound her zeal; that nothing but the confines of the earth can limit her power of expansion ; that she alone has a right to be styled the Church of the Universe. I allude to the late Œcumenical Council of the Vatican. It would look as if God, in His wise providence, had reserved this worldwide vindication of her claim to this particular epoch, when the sects have affected to despoil her of it, or to share it with her. We shall not undertake to describe this magnificent scene ourselves ; we shall leave the description of it to those outside the fold, who cannot help expressing their involuntary admiration of it.

The hall of assemblage, the number of prelates, the mitred heads, the distant climes from which many of them came, the different tongues they spoke, the antiquity of the heritage they represented, the power of the unbroken unity that had brought them together, their submissive attitude in the presence of the Common Father—the Supreme Pontiff, their unanimous submission to his decree ; all this was sketched in eloquent and graphic language by the correspondents of several of the great daily papers of London who were in Rome at the time.

The *Standard*, alluding to it, says :—" In historic importance, in traditional dignity, in the splendour of associations that gather round its name, no assembly in the world, past or present, can pretend to compare with the great parliament of the Latin Church. The unbroken continuity of the history of that Church is undeniable, and uninterrupted descent from the Church founded by the Apostles renders this Council

. . . the immediate successor and representative, in a sense in which no other Council can rival its claims, of the Council of Nicea, if not of the Council of Jerusalem. Nor is its actual power and consequence unworthy of its traditional heritage. It is the representative assembly, the omnipotent legislature, of a compact, coherent body of Christians, whose number approaches more nearly to two than to one hundred millions." After referring to the attempts made to hinder the Council, the correspondent adds:—" Nevertheless, all has been in vain, and the dispassionate observer is compelled to confess that the spectacle of so many hundreds of bishops, coming from the farthest quarters of the globe, at the beck of an old man, powerless in all but spiritual thunderbolts, is one that, occurring in the nineteenth century, and especially at this period of it, is calculated to strike the believing with pious admiration, and even the incredulous, like ourselves, with irrepressible astonishment".

The *Daily News* says:—" It must be admitted that weak as is the temporal power of the Pope, no other prince could have assembled such a body as met to-day in the council hall of St. Peter's, and no other could have provided them with such a magnificent temple. From the remotest quarters of the globe, from a land that was just heard of when the Council of Trent sat, from a land that was then wholly unknown, from Palestine and Syria, the cradles of Christianity, from Persia, from China, from India, from Africa, from the Western Isles, as well as from the countries washed by the Mediterranean, men of various tongues, of diverse origin, men of great learning and great age have come together to this famous city in obedience, voluntary and spiritual obedience, to the pastor who claims to be the successor of St. Peter, and the vicegerent of God upon earth."

Such is the testimony even of those who were not of her fold. Well, indeed, might it be said that that scene was one which was calculated to inspire the believing with "pious admiration, and even the incredulous with irrepressible astonishment". For what other Christian denomination in the world could reveal to the eyes of man a representation of universality, or rather a representation of universal unity, to compare with that which forced these words of glowing eulogium from the pen of hostile writers? The extension and duration of even the oldest and most widely-spread of other Churches dwindle into absolute insignificance when viewed side by side with the prestige, the venerable antiquity, universal diffusion, limitless dominion of the Church of Rome. No sectarian Church within the British Isles or beyond them can lay any claim to uniform universality in the face of this overpowering, unanswerable fact—a fact which no amount of sophistry can explain away—the fact of a world-wide diffusion of a Church, which is the same everywhere from sunrise to sunset, and whose identity with the Church of the Apostles is clearly traceable through all the centuries that have intervened between their day and our own. This fact alone, in the judgment of all calm, impartial, reasonable, sincere inquirers, ought to be sufficient to show that in her alone has been realised that undivided luminous universality which must ever distinguish the true Church of Christ—a universality which does not require that she should be found in every part of the globe simultaneously, but which *does* require that in every spot where she *is* found she should be one and the same.

I will close my remarks on this note of her truth by a brief allusion to her superiority of numbers, and to her perpetual, exclusive, inalienable possession of the title Catholic. The investigation of both points can only tend to give additional strength to her claims, and to mark her out as the one great religious body in the world which is beyond the reach of rivalry.

As a matter of fact the Catholic Church, in point of numbers, is far ahead, not merely of the most numerous of all the sectarian Churches throughout the world, but of all the sectarian Churches throughout the world collectively. All other Churches are confined within their own state and tributaries. The Church of England, which is the largest and the most influential of them all, both in a social and political point of view, is merely co-extensive with the British Empire, and contrives to subsist only under the protection of the British flag. The Catholic Church, on the other hand, is the Church of Europe, of Asia, of Africa, of America, of Australia, of the world. Lord Macaulay, in his essay on Ranke's *History of the Popes*, states that all Christian denominations outside the Catholic Church hardly reach a hundred and twenty millions. According to some writers, all the

Protestant denominations, even taken collectively, are estimated at sixty-five millions, or less than one-fifth of those who bear the Christian name. Considered as separate communions they are merely a handful. The members of the Greek schismatical Churches are supposed to number a little over seventy millions.

According to others, who are anxious to make their numbers look as large as possible, the aggregate of those professing non-Catholic Christian creeds, including the Oriental Churches, Protestantism, and all other sectarianisms, reaches a little beyond a hundred and thirty-one millions. But even the bitterest enemies of the Catholic Church—those who are most interested in depreciating her numbers and in swelling their own —freely admit that her members outnumber by many millions the members of all other Christian denominations put together. The *Tablet*, in its issue of October 17, 1885, gives the latest estimate of her numbers in the following words :—" The question of the number of Catholics throughout the world has been frequently discussed doth in these columns and elsewhere. We now have it, on the authority of the *Osservatore Romano*, that it results from the estimates made by the various missionaries that the total number of the members of the Catholic Church is actually between two hundred and seventy-five and three hundred millions."

But, as I have said already, on this majority of numbers I do not wish to insist. We have enough and more than enough to vindicate for her the mark of exclusive universality without it, as I have shown above.

Then, she alone possesses the title " Catholic," or
' Universal " ; and possession is nine-tenths of the law.
How came she to have sole possession of that title, if
any other Church deserved it better, if any other deserved it equally well, if any other deserved it at all ?
That she has verified the title, that is, that she has
been the teacher of the nations throughout all time,
since the days of the Apostles, we have already shown ;
that she alone has possessed the title itself from the
beginning is evident from history.

I will only give two or three citations from the early
Fathers. Such citations can be easily found in abundance ; but to introduce them at any length would
swell this little book beyond the contemplated limits.

In the first century, it is said of St. Polycarp, that
he used constantly to offer up prayers for the members
" of the Catholic Church diffused throughout the
world " (Euseb., *Hist. Ec.*, lib. iv., c. xv.).

Three centuries later St. Cyril, one of the greatest
Doctors of the Greek Church, and Patriarch of Jerusalem, instructed the faithful thus : " Should you come
into a city, do not inquire merely for the house of
God, for so heretics call their place of meeting ; nor
yet ask merely for the Church ; but say, the *Catholic*
Church—for this is the proper name" (*Catech.*, xviii.,
n. 26, p. 729).

In the same century, St. Pacianus, one of the lights
of the Latin Church, speaks in exactly the same tone :
" In the time of the Apostles, you will say, no one
was called *Catholic*. Be it so ; but when heresies
afterwards began, and, under different names, attempts

were made to disfigure and divide our holy religion, did not the apostolic people require a name, whereby to mark their unity, a proper appellation to distinguish their head? Accidentally entering a populous city, where are Marcionites, Novatians, and others who call themselves Christians, how shall I discover where my own people meet, unless they be called Catholics? I may not know the origin of the name; but what has not failed through so long a time came not surely from any individual man. It has nothing to say to Marcion, nor Appelles, nor Montanus. No heretic is its author. Is the authority of apostolic men, of the blessed Cyprian, of so many aged Bishops, so many martyrs and confessors, of little weight? Were not they of sufficient consequence to establish an appellation which they always used? Be not angry, my brother: Christian is my name, Catholic is my surname" (*Ep.* 1, *ad Sympronian Bib. PP. Max.*, t. iv., p. 729).

St. Epiphanius, a writer of the Greek Church, relates that, at Alexandria, those schismatics who adhered to Meletius styled their Church "the Church of the Martyrs," while the rest retained for theirs the name of "the Catholic Church" (*Hæres.*, tom. i., p. 719).

But no one has spoken more clearly or more emphatically on the point than St. Augustine. Here are his words :—"It is our duty," he says, " to hold to the Christian religion, and the *communion* of that Church which is called Catholic, and is so called, not by us only, but by all its adversaries. For whether they be so disposed or not, in conversing with others, they must use the word Catholic, or they will not be understood" (*De vera Religione*, c. vii., t. i., p. 752). He adds :—"Among the many considerations that bind me to the Church is the name of *Catholic*, which, not without reason, in the midst of so many heresies, *this Church alone has so retained*, that although all heretics wish to acquire the name, should a stranger ask where the Catholics assemble, the heretics will not dare to point out any of their own places of meeting" (*Contra Ep. Fundam.*, c. iv., tom. viii., 153).

So was it in the days of St. Augustine ; so is it now. The test which was used in his time, and which had been used for long years before it, holds good even at the present day. Go through the streets of London, Liverpool, Dublin, Belfast, Glasgow, Edinburgh—of any city through the length and breadth of Christendom— ask your way to the nearest Catholic Church, and he whom you ask, whether he be Methodist, Presbyterian, Protestant, or even the most advanced " Romanistic " Ritualist, will never think of directing you to one of his own conventicles, however stately and magnificent the building may be ; he will direct you to some church which is known to be in communion with the See of Rome. If he directs you otherwise, he feels that he is going against his conscience, and that he is leading you astray.

Every effort on the part of the sects, both in the past and in the present, to wrest this title from the Church of Rome, to appropriate it, or share it with her, has failed ignominiously. Those Ritualists and High Churchmen who designate themselves, and seek to be called, Catholics, often draw upon themselves the ridicule of other members of the Establishment.

However, what I have said of superiority of numbers, I say also with regard to the possession of the title *Catholic*—*i.e.*, I will not take advantage of it. I do not desire to insist at any length upon it. But what I *do* wish to insist upon chiefly and emphatically, above all and beyond all, is this : The Church of Christ exists somewhere on earth. Wherever she is and whatever she is, she must have the capacity of universal extension. No Church which has not the power of universal extension can be the Church of Christ. No Church can ever have the power of universal extension, except a Church which has a bond of unity springing from a necessary, unfailing principle of unity. And no Church on earth has, or claims to have, that necessary, unfailing bond of unity except the Roman Catholic Church. Therefore she alone can be the one true Church of Christ.

In her alone we find fulfilled these words of prophecy, which, in the belief not merely of those who profess her creed, but in the belief of almost all who belong to any denomination calling itself Christian, point to the Kingdom or Church of Christ : " All the ends of the earth shall remember, and shall be converted to the Lord, and all the kindred of the Gentiles shall adore in His sight ; for the kingdom is the Lord's, and He shall have dominion over the nations" (*Psalm* xxi. 28). "Ask of me, and I will give thee the Gentiles for thy inheritance, and the uttermost parts of the earth for thy possession" (*Psalm* ii.). "Of the increase of His government and peace there shall be no end, upon the throne of David, and upon His kingdom, to order it, and to establish it with judgment and with justice, from henceforth even and for ever" (Protestant Translation, *Isa.* ix. 7). "Upon thy walls, O Jerusalem, I have appointed watchmen all the day and all the night: they shall never hold their peace. You that are mindful of the Lord, hold not your peace" (*Isa.* lxii. 6). "Thy gates shall be open continually: they shall not be shut day nor night, that the strength of the Gentiles may be brought unto thee, and their kings may be brought" (*Isa.* lx. 11). "From the rising of the sun to the going down thereof, My name is great among the Gentiles: and in every place there is sacrifice, and there is offered to My name a clean oblation; for My name is great among the Gentiles, saith the Lord of Hosts" (*Mal.* i. 11).

Eliminate the Church in communion with Rome from history and from the world, and these prophetic utterances never have had, and never can have, a fulfilment.

Section IV.

Of course, when I say that the Christianity of all the nations of the earth, which have ever professed Christianity, is traceable to the first Apostles and their disciples, or to the See of Peter, as its source, I am to be understood as speaking of full and perfect Christianity : not of mutilated and corrupted Christianity.

From the beginning there have been corruptions of the Gospel. As there were heretics in the first century, so there have been heretics in every century since. And as heresiarchs had a certain following even in the days of the first Apostles, it is not surprising that the heresiarchs who came later should have a certain following too. If there were a few teachers of error in the early Church, while her numbers were still so small, how can we wonder there were more as her dominion extended, and as her members multiplied? When some went out of her and remained out of her, because they were not of her, even in her infancy, when she was still confined within comparatively narrow limits, and while the first heralds of her faith were living to guide, and guard, and defend her, and to confirm the truth of her teaching by their miracles, we are not to be astonished that others should go out of her in succeeding ages, when the sound of her voice had gone to the ends of the earth, and her children had become countless as the sands of the seashore.

On the contrary, we should rather be astonished if such had not been the case. For had no schisms and heresies arisen within her, as time went on, her history would have been entirely different from what the Apostles foretold it was to be. Those Apostles, so far from holding out assurances that the whole people of every nation, without exception, would receive her Gospel, and come within, and *remain*

within, her fold, and that she was never to have any
enemies or any rivals, and that her course throughout
was to be calm, smooth, prosperous, and free from all
opposition, predicted things far different. They predicted, in fact, that condition of things which has been
realised throughout her whole history. "I know,"
says St. Paul, "that after my departure ravenous
wolves will enter in among you, not sparing the flock.
And of your own selves will arise men speaking per-
verse things, to draw away disciples after them" (*Acts*
xx. 29, 30). And describing the character of heretics
of distant times, he says: "Know also this, that
in the last days shall come dangerous times; men
shall be lovers of themselves, stubborn, puffed up,
having the appearance indeed of godliness"—that is,
of genuine faith—"but denying the power thereof.
. . . But evil men and seducers shall grow worse
and worse, erring and driving into error. . . .
There shall be a time when they will not endure
sound doctrine; but according to their desires they
will heap to themselves teachers having itching ears"
(2 *Tim.* ii. and iii.). To the same Timothy he writes:
"Now the spirit manifestly saith that in the last
times some shall depart from the faith, giving heed to
spirits of error and doctrines of devils, speaking lies
in hypocrisy, and having their consciences seared"
(1 *Tim.* iv. 1, 2). And to the Corinthians he writes:
"For there must be also heresies, that they also, who
are approved, may be manifest among you" (1 *Cor.*
ii. 19).

The Apostles felt that the aggressive, laborious,

unyielding life of the Church in their own day was an index to her history to the end of time. They preached the faith, used all their powers to spread it. They were opposed by Simonians, Corinthians, Ebionites, heretics of various kinds, who rose up around them on all sides. They condemned those teachers of error in their separate individual warnings to the faithful. They called a council and condemned error again with united voice. They strove to fix the eyes of the Church's children everywhere on these decrees of condemnation. And having done this, they continued to preach and to work in spreading the faith farther and farther, with as much zeal and vigour, as if nothing had been done, or were *being* done, to thwart them in their efforts. In their mind this state of things indicated, symbolised what was to be the state of things in the Church down to the consummation. They knew that heresies must come; they knew also that those heresies could not prevent the Church from spreading; and they knew moreover that whether those heresies were to assume large proportions or small, were to cover half the earth or to be confined within some corner of it—whether they were to last for centuries, or to form, break, and disappear like a bubble—that all this was quite accidental, that they could never in any case be an argument against her Catholicity, no more than the heresies which appeared in their own day were an argument against it.

Looking at things from this apostolic standpoint, we see clearly the truth of the following statements :—

1. The fact that the influence of the Novation heresy in the third century extended from Rome to Scythia, to Asia Minor, to Africa, to Spain, proves nothing against the Catholicity of the Church.

2. The fact that the Donatists in the fourth century increased so rapidly in numbers and importance, that in a short time they had got possession of four hundred Episcopal Sees, and that all Africa for a period seemed to groan under the weight of Donatism, proves nothing against the Catholicity of the Church.

3. The fact that the followers of Arius converted the Gothic race to Arian Christianity; that they succeeded in inoculating Maesogoths, Visigoths, Ostrogoths, Alani, Suevi, Vandals, Burgundians, with their errors; that they succeeded, too, in spreading those errors through parts of France, Spain, Portugal, and Italy, and that those errors continued to be professed by numerous disciples in some of those countries for nearly a hundred years, and in others for nearly two hundred years, proves nothing against the Catholicity of the Church.

4. The fact that Nestorius, in the fifth century, went out of the Church, and induced many others to go out of her and to remain out of her; that his heresy was embraced and supported by some of the oldest Churches in Christendom; that it secured the protection of Persia; that it spread from Cyprus to China; that it was taken up by Indians, Medes, Huns, Bactrians; that it enlarged its dominion, and increased in numbers and importance till it possessed twenty-five archbishoprics; that it had a large portion of

Asia all to itself; that, according to the opinion of some, its members, united to those of the Monophysite heresy, at one time outnumbered the whole Catholic Church both in the East and the West; that, from its principal seat in Chaldea, it sent out missioners who worked with an activity and success that brought not merely many illustrious personages, but even some nations under its sway; that it held its ground in its varying forms for more than eight hundred years; and that during that long period it succeeded in preventing Catholic missioners from interfering much with the countries of which it had taken possession—even all this proves nothing against the Catholicity of the Church.

For, in the first place, all this was but a recurrence in later times, and on a wider scale when the Church was larger, of what had taken place even in the first century, when she was smaller, and when her first Apostles were still living. Nay, it was but a fulfilment of the Apostles' own predictions.

Secondly, our opponents as well as ourselves regard Novatians, Donatists, Arians, Nestorians, as heretics; and hence the imposing numbers and the wide diffusion of these rebellious bodies over the earth could be no proof of the truth of the doctrines which they taught.

But apart from this we must look at the matter from another point of view. The fact that Novatians, Donatists, Arians, Nestorians, and other heretics worked hard in spreading their errors does not prove that the Church in communion with Rome did not work equally hard in spreading the truth. *Their* activity is no proof of *her inactivity*. And in order that their labours and successes should be an argument against her claim to Catholicity, it would be necessary to show that, while *they*, during several centuries, were so energetic, *she*, during the same centuries, was idle and apathetic—looked on with folded arms, and made no effort either to dissipate their errors or to propagate her own doctrines more widely.

Well then, open history, and it will reveal to you that, while those world-wide heresies rose up and arrayed themselves against her, and strove like Antichrists to supplant her, she was constantly at work in pulling down and raising up, in breaking heresy to pieces and in building up the citadel of truth, in calling her bishops from the remotest parts to sit in council, to judge error and to condemn it, in notifying her decrees to the faithful throughout the world, in exerting her power to the utmost to have those decrees observed, and in sending her light to the most distant regions of the earth ; and that light shone everywhere except in those lands which shut their eyes against it, or, through the intrigues of heresy, refused to accept it.

Such had been her constant and untiring activity, that in spite of the ceaseless war heresy had waged against her, and in spite of the pagan persecutions which had sought to stamp her out, she had, by the end of the third and the beginning of the fourth century, propagated the faith—that is, *orthodox Christianity*—in the West, in Italy, in Proconsular Africa, in Numidia, in Mauritania, and even among the primitive Africans. *i.e.*, the Getuli and the Moors, who inhabited the interior of the country in the gorges and valleys of the Atlas, in Spain, in Gaul, in Upper and Lower Germany, along the borders of the Danube, in Norica (the modern Austria), in Vindelicia (the modern Bavaria), in Rhetia (at present the Tyrol). That faith had reached Britain also through Roman colonies which had gone there in the reign of Claudius. On the shores of the Mediterranean, in Thrace, Heminontis, Rhodope, Scythia, and Lower Mœsia, flourishing Churches had been established. In Macedonia, Thessalonica, Philippi, Beræa, the Churches which had been founded by the Apostles and their disciples, through their unbroken communion with Rome, still maintained their first fervour. In Athens, the capital of Greece, and in Byzantium, which was soon to be the capital of the New Empire, the faith had long been propagated.

In the East, that faith had already spread from Jerusalem (still true to say, from St. Peter as from its source) over all the cities of Palestine, Phœnicia, and Syria. Cesarea, Palestine, Tyre, Sidon, Ptolemais, Berytus, Tripoli, Biblos, Seleucia, Apamea, Hieropolis, Samosata, Antioch, all had their Churches. At an early date Bozra in Roman Arabia, and Edessa in the Osrhœne, had received the Gospel. In Meso potamia and Chaldea the Churches of Amida, Nisibis, Seleucia, and Ctesiphon were celebrated. Asia Minor, which had been evangelised by St. Paul, had its illustrious Sees of Ephesus, Laodicea, Pergamos, Philadelphia, Thyatira, Tarsus, Mopsuesta, Smyrna, Iconium, Myra, Miletus, Antioch of Pisidia,

Corinth, Nice, Chalcedon. Christians too were found in multitudes in the isles of Crete, Cyprus, and the Archipelago. Numerous and flourishing Churches had been established in Armenia and even in Persia. Egypt, in which the faith had been propagated by St. Mark, who founded the Patriarchate of Alexandria, had so advanced that it was able to send to the Council of Nice the Bishops of Naucrates, Phtinontis, Pelusium, Panephysus, Memphis, and Heraclea. The Thebais, which was soon to produce such examples of heroic sanctity, had in the third century several Episcopal Sees, among them Antinoe, Hermopolis, and Lycopolis. In the Pentapolis, of which Ptolemais was the Metropolitan See, many bishoprics had been founded.

In the fourth and fifth centuries she continued her work of evangelising. While Donatism, Arianism, Pelagianism, Nestorianism, Eutychianism, were drawing away multitudes from her ranks, and marshalling them under their respective standards against her, she was actively engaged not merely in striving to stay the progress of their errors, in holding Provincial Councils, National Councils, General Councils, to condemn them, and in promulgating her anathemas through all parts of the earth; she was also vigorously engaged in spreading her light in those regions where it had not yet shone, or was shining but faintly.

Her conquests now (and they were conquests of great magnitude) extended far beyond the boundaries of the Roman empire. She spread her faith still more widely in Persia, although that kingdom was soon to become one of the strongholds of Nestorianism, and a little later was to become the prey of Mahometanism. She brought within her fold the Iberians, who inhabited a territory between the Black Sea and the Caspian, and which is now known as Georgia. The Abyssinians, whose faith was destined to be, at least for a time, firm and durable, and whose Metropolitan was to be the Bishop of Ethiopia, were added to her triumphs. She succeeded, too, in Christianising vast districts of India—I mean, districts of it where her Gospel had not yet reached. Nay, while her General Councils were examining, discussing, and condemning the heresies of the East, she was at the same time making numberless conversions in some of the most distant isles of the West. It was during that period that, through the zeal and labours of St. Patrick and his companions, she levelled the altars of the Druids in Ireland, cleared that country of every trace of paganism, and placed its people from shore to shore in possession of that full and perfect and uncorrupted Christianity which they have never lost. And not long afterwards she sent, under the guidance of Augustin, to Britain, the band of heroic missionaries who were destined to revive in that kingdom the faith of which it had almost been entirely despoiled in the persecution of Diocletian, or the practice of which, at least, had almost entirely ceased there.

Now, if Donatism, Arianism, Pelagianism, Nestorianism, Eutychianism, which occupied such vast portions of the globe, which counted such multitudes of disciples, and which exercised such sway for centuries, furnish no argument against the universality of the Church, it is difficult to see how any serious objection against her universality can be taken from the bulk of the Greek schismatical communions of the present day, or from the wide prevalence of Protestantism which has taken possession of so many countries, and which is professed by so many peoples. The Greek schismatics of the East, as well as the Protestants of the West, admit that the disciples of these various religious bodies were heretics; and in admitting this they are virtually admitting that their own bulk and influence, in themselves, go no way either towards proving that they are members of the true Church, or towards proving that the claim of the Church of Rome is weakened or affected in any way through their vastness. This ought to be remembered by those to whom Cardinal Newman refers when he says:—"Bulk not symmetry, vastness not order, are their tests of truth".

But we may go further. The wide diffusion of Nestorianism, of the Greek schism, of the heresy of the Reformation, is no more an argument against the universality of the Catholic Church than is the wide and wonderful spread of Mahometanism; and the sway which Mahometanism exercised over so many millions for so many ages is no more an argument against that universality than are those numberless pagans who are outside the pale of Christianity altogether. "Corruptions of the Gospel," says Cardinal Newman again, "are as necessary and ordinary a phenomenon, taking men as they are, as its rejection. Is misbelief," he asks, "a greater marvel than unbelief? or do not the same intellectual and moral principles which lead men to accept nothing, lead them also to accept half of revealed truth? Both effects are simple manifestations of private judgment in the bad sense of the phrase, that is, of the use of one's own reason against the authority of God."

This is strikingly true. Heresy or schism, however widely spread, interferes no more with the universality of the Church than absolute infidelity. From the outset the Church was only one of a number of communions which professed to be Christian. From the days of the Apostles, true belief, misbelief, unbelief, have walked side by side. Among those who had the Gospel preached to them, some received it, some mutilated it, some rejected it. In the last (the twenty-eighth) chapter of the Acts, we find it stated that many came to the lodgings of St. Paul, that they might hear from him an account of the new religion; and that he expounded it to them at great length, " testifying the kingdom of God, and persuading them concerning Jesus, out of the law of Moses and the Prophets from morning to night ". And it is added that a certain number were persuaded, and that others were not persuaded. "Some believed the things that were said but some believed not " (*Acts* xxiii. 24). So was it then, so has it been ever since, so is it now, so will it be to the end of time. The Church's note of universality does not require it to be otherwise; that note is independent of all rejections, mutilations, corruptions of her Gospel. It does not rest on the condition that in every century *she* must have exclusive sway over three-fourths of the globe; or that in every generation nine out of ten of the world's population must profess her doctrine. It is not to be measured by mathematical lines. No. What is essential to it is that, wherever she exists, she should be found at all times and in all circumstances to be one and the same. And *that* she is found to be. In point of space, Rome, or the See of Peter, is her centre, the boundaries of the earth her only circumference. And, in point of identity, she is now what she was in the days of the Apostles, and what she is now she will continue to be to the end of time; for she is the one and only true Church of the unchanged, unchanging, and unchangeable God.

CONCLUSION.

THE theory of Indifferentism may help much, strange as it may sound to say so, in the search after the true Church. To realise this fully, we must fix our thoughts again for a moment on some of the many inconsistencies, incoherences, and endless contradictions with which that theory is pregnant.

And first of all, I would draw attention to this :— If God is indifferent in what sense men receive His revelation, it follows He is indifferent in what sense they receive His ten Commandments, since the ten Commandments are but a portion of His revelation. Now I assume that no one who pretends to be a Christian will hold that men are free to choose the contradictories of the Commandments as the standard of their morality. On what grounds, then, can it be affirmed that they are free to choose the contradictories of His revealed doctrines as the object of their faith? Where is the reason for making any difference? Does not such a system do away with the distinction between truth and falsehood altogether? Why should God promulgate a special precept forbidding lies, if every man was to be free to give to the precept itself two opposite interpretations—that is, to understand it either as forbidding people to state what is false, or as commanding them never to state anything else except what is false.

But we may put the thing in a stronger light still. The only reason why the Commandments are binding on the human conscience is because Revelation teaches that they are the expression of God's will in regard to man. Apart from this revealed teaching, they can have no obligatory power at all. Take away the Divine truth that there is one God, and one only—that He is the Creator, Sovereign Lord of all—that He is to be worshipped by His creatures, and the first Commandment is meaningless and without force. Put aside the doctrine, that He is infinitely powerful, infinitely wise, infinitely good—that He is all pure and all holy—that His name is, therefore, to be hallowed, and the second Commandment ceases to bind. Cancel the revelation that our neighbour's soul is made to the Divine image—that it is the Divine will we should love him, and those commandments which refer to the duties of fraternal charity lose all their binding force. It is the doctrines on which they are founded that give to the Commandments their hold upon the will of man, and their claim to his obedience. And hence the only reason why we have no authority to change the Commandment is because we have no authority to change the doctrinal truth on which it rests. And if we have no leave or privilege to take opposite views of God's revelation in one case, how can we have any leave or privilege to take opposite views of it in another?

Again, if God inscribed His ten Commandments on tablets of stone, and had them preserved in the Ark that they might keep the form and meaning He originally gave them, and that He might show the high and important place which they occupied in His Divine mind, He surely intended there should be a means of preserving the doctrinal portion of His revelation in the sense and meaning it had at the outset. If He deigned to reveal certain truths of faith, it was because He meant them to be heard and to be believed, and if He meant them to be heard and to be believed, it was undoubtedly because He set some value upon them. But in what sense could they be said to have any value in His eyes, if He merely cast them out upon the world and let men treat them as they liked —allowing them to be looked upon as meaning anything, or as meaning nothing, or as meaning two contradictory things in one and the same moment? With what show of reason can it be maintained that He attached any importance to them at all, if He intended His people were to be at liberty to believe them or not to believe them, or to believe their opposites, or to believe anything else in their stead if they chose?

One of two things : either He never made a revelation at all, or, if He did, He cannot have left it to be the sport of men's whims and fancies. If He revealed certain doctrines to the world, it must have been with the intention that they should be not merely believed, but should be believed according to the meaning in which He revealed them. And the very same reason that would lead Him to reveal them would force Him to institute some means of making them always express the same sense, and of surrounding them with such guardianship as would render them secure against being tampered with by the ever-changing opinions, and idle, erring speculations of men.

When He took such care lest the precepts of the Decalogue should be changed, surely He must have taken quite as much care that the revelations made by His Divine Son should never be changed. And if that Divine Son Himself cleared and purged the Mosaic Law, which was to be made void, of the false traditions and interpretations of the Scribes and Pharisees, would He not take precautions lest similar false interpretations might be introduced in the course of time into the laws and doctrines which He Himself revealed for all ages. The revelations to which He referred in the words of the great commission were, to say the least, quite as important as those delivered to Moses on Mount Sinai. And doubtless those revelations of His New Dispensation, which He condescended to make to the world with His own lips, would have been committed to stone also, had He not designed to preserve their identity and sense by a guardianship still more sacred, of which we shall speak presently—that is, His own special help, His own special presence, His own personal supervision, nay, His own unerring voice ever speaking through His Church, which He meant to be His mouth-piece on earth throughout all time.

And now this opens out a new view of the matter before us—a view which, on the one hand, reveals clearly the hollow fallacies of Indifferentism ; and which, on the other hand, brings out into striking prominence the irresistible claims of the Catholic Church to be the sole authorised, adequate, infallible guardian and teacher of all revealed truth.

The very fact that Indifferentists disagree among themselves, not merely about things which they take the unwarrantable liberty of terming *minor* points of revelation, but disagree also as to *what doctrines are to be regarded as the fundamental doctrines* of Christianity—this, I may say, of itself is sufficient to establish two things : first, the unreasonableness and utter untenableness of their system, and, secondly, the necessity of an authoritative voice *still speaking* which can tell with certainty what has been revealed and what has not.

Let us dwell on this for a moment. The adherents of Indifferentism differ even as to what are those truths which are to be deemed essentials, the peculiar doctrines, the vital doctrines, the leading idea, the great truth, of the Gospel. Some say that it is the

Divinity of Christ, some the Redemption, some the Resurrection, some that Divine Charity is everything, and some that the immortality of the human soul is the essence of the Gospel, and all that need be believed. They dispute over almost every doctrine which is spoken of as lying within the sphere of revelation. And hence their system, when taken to pieces, plainly means that God once, or at sundry times, revealed a number of doctrines with the design they should be believed, and that at the same time He left His people perfectly free to affirm or to deny every one of those truths from beginning to end, according as they thought proper. Is not this equivalent to saying that He made a revelation, and that it was utterly useless to make it, since men were quite as wise before it was made as after they received it?

But this is not all. The fact, that Indifferentists take opposite views about even the *vital doctrines* of Christianity, is not only a refutation of their theory, it is at the same time proof sufficient; it compels us to the conclusion that if God ever vouchsafed to make a revelation to the world, He must have consigned it to such careful keeping as would preserve it always in its entirety, and make it always express exactly the same thing. Why should He reveal a doctrine, unless He wished it to have always the same meaning? How could He wish it to have always the same meaning, if He intended, when He revealed it, that men were to be at liberty to give it any interpretation they chose? And how could men at any time be certain of its *true* meaning unless there were to be from age to age an authoritative, definitive, infallible voice to *tell* its meaning?

Unless there exist some such unerring authority on earth, there can never be any certainty about revealed doctrine of any kind, whether it be called fundamental or non-fundamental. Nay, there can never be any certainty even that those doctrines which are said to be revealed have been revealed at all. And what is more, if that unerring voice spoke only during the first two or three, or four or five, or six or seven centuries, and then became silent, and has never spoken since, how can there be any certainty now about those truths which ought to form the object of faith? Unless it speaks still, even at the present moment, it is impossible to make an act of faith at all. For faith supposes certainty and excludes doubt: faith is incompatible with doubt, and undoubting faith I can never have, unless I regard as infallible the voice which teaches me what I am to believe.

Yet our Lord makes faith an essential condition of salvation; and the Apostle tells us that without faith it is impossible to please God. Now, would God make faith a necessary qualification for entrance into heaven, and then leave men in the impossibility of ever possessing it, of ever exercising it, of ever eliciting an act of it? In such a plight He must have left them, unless there is in the world some source of *unquestionable* authority which can tell for certain what has been revealed, how much has been revealed, what its true meaning, and in what sense it is to be received.

Cardinal Manning, in his book, *Temporal Missiou of the Holy Ghost*, refers to this point :—" There are some who appeal from the voice of the living Church to antiquity, professing to believe that while the Church was united it was infallible, that then when it became divided it ceased to speak infallibly, and that the only certain rule of faith is to believe that which the Church held and taught while yet it was united, and therefore infallible. Such reasoners fail to observe that since the supposed division, and cessation of the infallible voice, there remains no Divine certainty as to what was then infallibly taught."

If it be urged that the Scriptures contain all the truths of revelation, the state of the case is not altered. The same reasoning holds good : for I answer how can I be sure that the Scriptures, as they are now published, are identical with the Scriptures of the fourth and fifth centuries, unless an infallible authority tells me they are ? How can I be sure they contain the Word of God at all, unless the same infallible authority tells me they do ? How can I be sure whether the Catholic version or the Protestant is the correct one—the one that contains the truth, and nothing but the truth—unless I regard as infallible the decision of my informant ? If the authority which tells me that the Old and New Testaments are the Word of God be a fallible authority, and therefore a questionable one, then, whether it is the voice of an individual or the voice of a hundred millions of individuals, I can have no certainty, and consequently cannot exercise faith. For the opinions of a fallible multitude, equal in number to the whole population of the earth, as long as there is question of the things which are beyond the reach of reason, can never produce certainty of any kind, much less absolute, infallible certainty.

But granting that the Scriptures contain the whole truth and nothing but the truth, and putting aside the question which version is the right one, let us test the matter on another ground. How can I be sure which is the true interpretation of those passages, from which are drawn contradictory doctrines with regard to points which are commonly called points of fundamental importance—such, for example, as the passages which refer to the Eucharistic presence and sacramental confession—unless I have an infallible teacher to guide, enlighten, and instruct me?

I think then we are warranted in drawing the conclusion, that if God ever came into the world for the purpose of making a revelation and of instituting a Church, He must have established an unerring interpreter of the one and an unfailing ruler of the other, since there was exactly the same reason for instituting a means of protecting the revelation against false meanings, as there was for making the revelation at all. To have acted otherwise would have been to defeat His own ends; for either He intended His revealed doctrines to have contradictory meanings, or He did not. If He did, then He changes, and He is the God of truth to-day and the God of lies to-morrow; or He is the God of truth and of lies in one and the same moment, for the same individual, and under the very same circumstances. If He did *not* intend them to have contradictory meanings, then He cannot have abandoned them to every chance interpretation and to every human caprice. He must have raised up around them ramparts of defence which would protect them against the encroachment of innovation, and prevent their being wrecked by the ever-varying judgments and wandering imaginations of men. Yes, being the unchanged, unchanging, and unchangeable God, the same yesterday, to-day, and. for ever, He must have established on earth an undying authority, whose infallible voice would speak in His name throughout all the vicissitudes of time and throughout the coming and passing away of all generations down to the day of doom—an authority whose voice would proclaim to the world, with unerring certainty, those doctrines which He revealed, and *those only*, and declare to all men the sense in which they were to be understood.

Either this must be granted, or a system of faith there cannot be, since otherwise absolute certainty about the object of faith there cannot be.

Well then, dear reader, raise your eyes, look around you, inquire, examine. Is there any Church on earth in which this unerring authority is found—in which this infallible voice speaks? Where is it? Which is it?

One and one only claims it. It is that one which alone can give sufficient reason for urging the claim —the one which, from her mark of everlasting, undivided unity, and from her inborn power of universal expansion, we have shown to be the one only true Church of the living God on this earth.

APPENDIX.

1.—The advocates of Indifferentism may be inclined to think that I have put my arguments in too concrete a form. My defence is—If a theory cannot stand the test of analysis in the concrete, it cannot be held to be capable of standing that test in the abstract; and if it cannot stand the test of analysis either in the abstract or the concrete, it is clear it cannot stand such test at all.

2.—With regard to the passage which I have introduced from St. Irenæus in page 126, in reference to the Supremacy of the Roman See, and to the necessity of being in communion with that See, the meaning will be still more clear in the translation of the words found in Father Ryder's admirable book, *Catholic Controversy*, page 14. It is as follows:—" For with this Church (the Church of Rome) it is necessary that every Church—that is, the Faithful on every side—should be in communion, in which has ever been preserved by the Faithful everywhere that tradition which is from the Apostles ".

A portion of the same passage is thus translated by Cardinal Wiseman :—" To this Church (See of Rome), ON ACCOUNT OF ITS SUPERIOR HEADSHIP, every other must have recourse—that is, the Faithful of all countries ". Every faithful translation brings out prominently the SOVEREIGN SUPREMACY OF THE SEE OF ST. PETER AND THE IMPERIOUS NECESSITY OF BEING IN COMMUNION WITH IT.

3.—In pages 222-224 I state that unless some infallible voice speaks still it is impossible to make an act of faith. Lest I should be misunderstood, I wish to add : If Protestants can make an act of faith, it is not AS PROTESTANTS, *or while resting on the principles of Protestantism*, they can make it. No ; but it is because they believe implicitly in an infallible authority without professing or pretending to believe in it—that is, THEY place infallibility in the dead letter of Scripture, while *Catholics* place it in the living voice of the living Teacher. In other words, if they can make an act of faith, it is because they implicitly accept the historical testimony and infallible teaching of the Catholic Church that the Scriptures are the Inspired Word of God.

Had the space, beyond which I was determined not to go, permitted, I should have treated this point, as well as some others, at much greater length. From the outset I meant this book to be of such size that people might be able to read it in the spare hours of a few evenings, or at all events in the spare evenings of a few Sundays, and I also meant it to appear at such price as would bring it within easy reach of all.

Letters from His Grace the Secretary of the Propaganda, and of His Grace the Archbishop of Ephesus, Rector of the Irish College, Rome, to Father MacLaughlin, on the occasion of the presentation of his book. "Indifferentism; or, Is one Religion as good as Another?" to the Holy Father.

ROME—IRISH COLLEGE.

REV. DEAR FATHER,
4th January, 1889.

I feel great pleasure in informing you that I had your able work on Religious Indifferentism presented to the Holy Father through the kindness of His Grace the Secretary of Propaganda, and that His Holiness was pleased to accept it with expressions of benevolence and approbation for your most useful labours in defence of our holy religion. These sentiments of His Holiness towards yourself and your zeal for the cause of Catholic truth, the above-mentioned Secretary, Monsignor Jacobini, was pleased to express in the enclosed letter to yourself.

Please accept my best thanks for the copy you sent me of your invaluable book, which I greatly value, and for which I desire an extensive circulation, as its perusal cannot fail to dissipate the errors which unfortunately too widely prevail on the importance of the profession of the faith, without which the Apostle declares it impossible to please God—the *one* faith "una fides"—which only exists in the Church which Christ founded and placed under the supreme guidance of St. Peter and his successors to the end of time by the memorable words: "Feed My lambs, feed My sheep".

I remain, REV. DEAR FATHER,

Yours sincerely in Christ,

✠ T. KIRBY,
Archbishop of Ephesus, Rector.

REV. JOHN MACLAUGHLIN.

The following is the translation of the Letter of His Grace the Secretary of Propaganda:—

ROME, *22nd December*, 1888.

SACRED CONGREGATION OF THE PROPAGANDA.

On the occasion of the presentation to the Holy Father of the book on Religious Indifferentism.

REV. DEAR FATHER,

It is a very great pleasure to me to be able to make known to you that I have presented to the Holy Father the book lately written by you on Religious Indifferentism, and that His Holiness not merely graciously accepted it with expressions of benevolence, but also spoke in terms of high praise of the zeal and earnestness with which you write in defence of religion.

With feelings of deep esteem, I subscribe myself, yours most affectionately,

✠ D., *Archbishop of Tyre.*

REV. JOHN MACLAUGHLIN.

APPROBATIONS.

From His Eminence, the Most Rev. HENRY EDWARD CARDINAL MANNING, *Archbishop of Westminster.*

"Your little book seems to me very sound and safe, and it cannot fail, I think, to be useful. I shall gladly recommend it."

From His Eminence, the Most Rev. JOHN HENRY CARDINAL NEWMAN.

"I have been reading your book since it came to me with great interest and pleasure, and pray and trust it may achieve that success which you desire for it, and which it deserves."

From His Eminence, the Most Rev. CARDINAL MORAN.

"I have received the copy of your excellent book which you so kindly sent me. It contains a great deal in comparatively small space; and is therefore particularly well suited to the taste of readers of the present generation, who do not care to peruse large books. . . . They wish to find much said and well said within short compass. . . . This accounts for the rapid sale of your admirable work. I am taking a number of copies with me to Sydney.
"Written from Rome, July, 1888."

From His Eminence, the Most Rev. JAMES CARDINAL GIBBONS, *Archbishop of Baltimore.*

"I intend to have a notice of your admirable little book inserted in the Baltimore *Catholic Mirror*."

From the Most Rev. W. SMITH, *Archbishop of Edinburgh.*

"I am delighted to hear that you are contemplating a second edition of your invaluable little book on 'Indifferentism'. Your reasoning is so clear and cogent, that it ought to convince every candid mind, and the kindly tone that pervades it must recommend itself to all. I trust it may have a large circulation."

From the Most Rev. CHARLES EYRE, D.D., *Archbishop of Glasgow.*

"I write to thank you very much, indeed, for the copy you have sent me of your book. Twice I have read it, and with increasing interest. The two illustrations from the history of Cornelius, page 51, and from Count Stolberg, page 109, are very telling. It must bring home consolation to very many. Some days ago I sent a copy to a friend, who is in search of the truth, and this book may cause the person to cross the Rubicon."

From the Most Rev. MICHAEL CORRIGAN, D.D., *Archbishop of New York.*

"I have spoken of your book to Benziger Bros., and have asked them to do their best for its circulation here."

From the Most Rev. PATRICK RYAN, D.D., *Archbishop of Philadelphia.*

"Please to accept my thanks for your work on 'Indifferentism,' which you have been kind enough to send me. It is an excellent book, and I trust it will find circulation in this country, where it is much needed."

From the Most Rev. THOMAS PORTER, S.J., *Archbishop of Bombay.*

"I am much obliged to you for the copy of your book, 'Is one Religion as good as another?' I will do what I can to spread it in India. I have read it and can conscientiously say you have given us a useful popular book on a most important practical question. This day's mail will carry to you a number of *The Bombay Catholic Examiner*, containing a review of the book."

From the Most Rev. PATRICK RIORDAN, D.D., *Archbishop of San Francisco.*

"I beg leave to acknowledge the receipt of your book 'Indifferentism,' for which please accept my sincere thanks. I had ordered it some weeks ago through a local bookseller. I shall not have time to read it till after the Christmas holidays. But judging from the favourable notices of the press, I am confident that it will prove to be a most excellent work to give to those who are seeking the true Church.—San Francisco, Dec., 1887."

From the Most Rev. WILLIAM VAUGHAN, D.D., *Bishop of Plymouth.*

"I think your book is calculated to do much good. It is certainly very crushing to that spirit of 'Indifferentism,' so prevalent in all classes at the present day, and I hope it will enable many to find their way into the true fold. God bless you and your work."

From the Most Rev. ROBERT CORNTHWAITE, D.D., *Bishop of Leeds.*

"I have read your book and think it is calculated to do great good. May God bless you and it."

From the Most Rev. HERBERT VAUGHAN, D.D., *Bishop of Salford.*

"I am very much obliged for the copy you have so kindly sent me of your work on 'Indifferentism'. I trust it will have a steady and permanent sale. I wish you every blessing, and desire for your works a great fruitfulness."

From the Most Rev. JOHN CUTHBERT HEDLEY, O.S.B., *Bishop of Newport and Menevia.*

"I thank you very much for the copy of 'Indifferentism' you were good enough to send me. As far as I have been able to judge, it is a book which will prove extremely useful both to the general public, and to priests in particular."

From the Most Rev. EDMUND KNIGHT, D.D., *Bishop of Shrewsbury.*

"I am reading your little volume with intense interest. *Rem tetigisti.* It deals with the practical question of the day. Would we could make it read by those who most need its teaching. As you say, some of our own would benefit by looking into it. I wish every success to your good work."

From the Most Rev. RICHARD LACY, D.D., *Bishop of Middlesbrough.*

"Pray accept my best thanks for your book on 'Indifferentism,' which I am reading with much interest and pleasure. There can be no doubt that broad liberalism in religion is the prevailing attitude of the millions in this country. . . . I fervently pray that your valuable book may be the means of restoring to freedom many who are yet in the bondage of error. It deserves to be read and re-read by the clergy, for it deals in an able and practical way with a most important subject. I will gladly use my influence towards the spread of it in whatever way I can."

From the Most Rev. JOHN BUTT, D.D., *Bishop of Southwark.*
(Through his Vicar-General, Canon Murnane.)

"His Lordship, the Bishop of Southwark, wishes me to thank you for your valuable work on 'Indifferentism'. Such a book, simply and forcibly written, was much needed, for beyond comparison, I think, the subject-matter of it is the evil of the day. Your work will be a useful manual to all who have a part in the great fight against the world."

From the Most Rev. JOHN VIRTUE, D.D., *Bishop of Portsmouth.*

"I am happy to be able to say that I have read your little book, every word of it. And in thanking you for it, I can add that I have read it with much pleasure, and I feel satisfied it will do no little good. I hope our Divine Lord will bless your efforts to extend His kingdom on earth."

From the Most Rev. JOHN MacDONALD, D.D., *Bishop of Aberdeen.*

"Allow me to thank you very much for the copy of your book on 'Indifferentism,' which is a very opportune publication. . . . I cannot, I feel sure, express a wish more agreeable to you in regard to this result of your labours, than that God may bless it, and render it productive of the best fruits in quarters where it was intended, and where they are much needed."

From the Most Rev. JOHN MacLAUGHLIN, D.D., *Bishop of Galloway.*

"Many thanks for your book. Every page I have read is replete with useful and interesting information, as well as solid reasoning. It seems also to be written, as it should be, in a style that will take with the public. I congratulate you on the result of your labours, and wish your work every success."

From the Most Rev. ANGUS MACDONALD, D.D., *Bishop of Argyll and the Isles.*

"I write to thank you for your book. It cannot fail to do good. I heartily wish it every success."

From the Most Rev. PATRICK M'ALLISTER, D.D., *Bishop of Down and Connor.*

"Your book, 'Indifferentism; or, Is one Religion as good as another?' has come as a timely antidote against a poison which threatens to infect the present age. No one can read it without being deeply impressed with the truth of the saying of our Divine Lord: 'He that is not for Me is against Me'. It deserves an honoured place in all parochial and Catholic libraries. I trust its circulation may be commensurate with its merits, and the good fruits which it is sure to produce in the minds of those who read it."

From the Most Rev. JOHN HEALY, D.D., *Coadjutor Bishop of Clonfert.*

"Your arguments are very solid, clear, and forcibly put; and I have no doubt that your book will do a vast amount of good."

From the Most Rev. JAMES BROWNE, D.D., *Bishop of Ferns.*

"I beg to acknowledge with thanks the receipt of your new work. I am sure it will have a most beneficial effect on the minds of many Protestants, who are not quite sure of the ground they are standing on. It will also do good to a certain class of Catholics."

From the Most Rev. WILLIAM WEATHERS, D.D., *Bishop of Amycla, Bishop Auxiliary to His Eminence Cardinal Manning.*

"On my return to London, after a considerable time of absence, I find a presentation copy of your little book on Indifference in matters of religion. The subject is one, more in England, perhaps, than anywhere else, of great importance. I have looked into your book, and think it very able as well as opportune, and shall be most glad to recommend the perusal of it."

OPINIONS OF THE PRESS.

From *The Whitehall Review* (Non-Catholic), London.—
" It is plain, straightforward, reasoning from stem to stern."
From *The Scottish Review Quarterly* (Non-Catholic).—" It is
deserving of the popularity it has attained." From *The
Spectator* (Non-Catholic), London.—" These discussions have
a great deal more coherence and relevance than any one who
judged of the treatise by the title would be at all disposed to
infer." From *The Graphic* (Non-Catholic), London.—" The
book is a forcible eulogy on Catholic oneness, contrasted with
the multifarious divisions of Protestantism." From *The Daily
Telegraph* (Non-Catholic), London.—" The argument is stated
clearly and forcibly." From *The Leader* (Non-Catholic),
London.—" His arguments are ably put and skilfully applied."
From *The Weekly Times and Echo* (Non-Catholic), London.—
" We must candidly confess that Mr. MacLaughlin seems to us
master of the situation if there is any one religion specially
revealed from heaven." From *The Scotsman* (Non-Catholic).
—" Plainer reasoning was never addressed to plain men." From
The Aberdeen Journal (Non-Catholic).—" Father MacLaughlin
has produced a very able book. His theory is very beautifully
wrought out." From *The North British or Glasgow Daily
Mail* (Non-Catholic).—" In certain parts of his argument
earnest evangelical Protestants may concur with him. The
tone of the book is kindly and earnest." From *The Glasgow
Evening News* (Non-Catholic).—" He reasons with great
cogency and the tone of the discussion throughout is remarkable for its temperance." From *The Scottish Leader* (Non-
Catholic).—" This is in many respects an interesting little
book." From *The Perthshire Advertiser* (Non-Catholic).—" In
the work of disproving from his point of view the claims of his
antagonists and rivals, he refrains from using sarcasm, or
irony, or disrespect." From *The Liverpool Daily Post* (Non-
Catholic).—" Is written with much graceful scholarship and
without bigotry." From *The Manchester Courier* (Non-
Catholic).—" The manner in which Mr. MacLaughlin con-
ducts a controversy is worthy of all praise." From *The Liverpool Daily Mercury* (Non-Catholic).—" He (the author) is well

known to the Catholic body as one of the most eloquent missionary preachers." From *The Observer* (Non-Catholic), London.—"The delicate and difficult question of religious differences is ably and judiciously handled by the Rev. J. MacLaughlin's instruction, and food for wholesome reflection may be found therein by all searchers after truth." From *The Leeds Mercury* (Non-Catholic).—"It manifests a kindliness of tone and freedom from bitterness, as well as an air of candour. The author is thoroughly attached to his Church, and writes in an honest and outspoken spirit, and in good flowing English." From *The Newcastle Leader* (Non-Catholic).—"Much will be found in it to suggest reflection, and not a little that will compel agreement." From *The Melbourne Leader* (Non-Catholic).—"May be read with equal appreciation in a Romish or a Wesleyan School." From *The Melbourne Australasian* (Non-Catholic).—"The author concentrates his strength on two or three principles, which are lucidly conceived, forcibly expressed and well argued." From *The Victorian Independent* (Non-Catholic), Melbourne.—"Its English almost equals that of Cardinal Newman at his best, and the spirit and tone pervading the volume are admirable." From *The Dominion Illustrated* (Non-Catholic), Montreal.—"Its acceptability to the British public is vouched for by the fact that it has reached its tenth thousand." From *The Christian Colonist* (Non-Catholic), Adelaide.—"He reasons with temperate language in a clear and forcible style." From *The Nihill and Latira Mail* (Non-Catholic), South Australia.—"The work will be found worthy of perusal." From *The Church Times* (Non-Catholic), London.—"He has said what can be said with a certain dexterity." From *The Dublin Review.*—"This is a book that is wanted." From *The Month*, London.—"The author of this little book has driven his bolt well home and shot true into the camp of his adversary." From *The Tablet.* —"It is not often we meet with a new book of religious controversy so satisfactory as that which is now before us." From *The Weekly Register*, London.—"The work is admirably produced and its popular edition ought to reach tens of thousands." From *The Catholic Times.*—"The reverend author of this much-needed work has thrown all the energy of his intellect and close reasoning into the answer 'No' to the question proposed in the title." From *The Universe*, London.— "We thank Father MacLaughlin for his very excellent and (at this day specially) most necessary work." From *The Glasgow Observer.*—"A most conclusive answer to the many who say in these days that one religion is as good as another." From *The Irish Ecclesiastical Record.*—"It has every condition necessary to render a book popular." From *The Irish*

Monthly.—" He treats his subject with a great deal of vigour, freshness, and originality." From *The Lyceum,* Dublin.—" It will appeal powerfully to the common-sense of all who will be wise enough to make a study of its pages." From *Freeman's Journal,* Dublin.—" It is written with precision and perspicuity, and there is not an unintelligible phrase throughout it." From *The Cork Examiner.*—" No man, we unhesitatingly say, can read, and provided only he is honest to his own heart, remain indifferent." From *United Ireland.*—" It is a plain matter of logic—clear, close-reasoned and clothed in simple yet graceful form." From *The Belfast Morning News.*—" We heartily welcome this work from the pen of the gifted missionary the Rev. John MacLaughlin." From *The American Catholic Quarterly Review.*—" This unpretentious and modest, but able little book is emphatically a ' Tract for the Times'." From *The Catholic World* (American).—" He has brought to his task a great store of accurate information, much good sense, and his missionary life guarantees a wide experience. His book, though it is not large or costly, is a repertory of well-chosen arguments." From *The Catholic Review* (American). —" In a small compass without effort, without dryness, in all simplicity and in an engaging tone and temper he has proved that Indifferentism is the master evil of the day. Catholic priests would find this book very useful as a handmaid to their own efforts in instructing Protestants." From *The Boston Pilot* (American).—" This book puts the right weapon in the hands of the children of the Church." From *The Catholic Universe,* Cleveland, Ohio, U.S.A.—" This is a charming book of 236 pages, and a most timely publication." From *The Catholic Book News* (American).—" I should strongly recommend this little book as a gift to all well-intentioned Protestants." From *The Catholic Book Talk* (American).—" *Is one Religion as good as Another?* is having a good sale and is just the book." From *The Catholic Telegraph* (American).— " Father MacLaughlin's work is a timely contribution on the subject." From *The Pittsburg Catholic* (American).—" No words are wasted, but every argument is advanced in striking conciseness and logical sequence." From *The North Western Chronicle,* St. Paul, Minn., America.—" Father MacLaughlin writes in a clear and forcible style." From *The Catholic Weekly* (American).—" To say the work is well done would not be doing justice to the learned author's labours." From *The Owl,* Ottawa (Canadian).—" Throughout the work the author shows himself an able philosopher, a deeply read historian, and a sound theologian." From *The North Western Review,* Winnipeg (Canadian).—" He puts before his readers the note of Catholicity in a way never before brought explicitly

under their notice." From *The Republic*, Boston (America).—
"The force of the author's logic cannot but make itself felt
even on prejudiced readers." From *The Pilot*, Boston (America).
—"Few recent works of the kind have attracted so much attention." From *The Bombay Catholic Examiner*.—"This little
book of the Rev. J. MacLaughlin is deserving of all praise."
From *The Indo-European*, Calcutta.—"Among the numerous
books supplied by the Catholic Truth Society is one to which,
as best suited to our times, we would fain call the attention of
our readers. We allude to *Indifferentism; or, is One Religion
as Good as Another?* by the Rev. J. MacLaughlin." From *The
Advocate*, Melbourne.—"It is very desirable that Father Mac-
Laughlin's work be placed at every opportunity in the hands
of our separated brethren." From *The Catholic Standard*,
Hobart, Tasmania.—"Father MacLaughlin has done good
service in exposing the delusion." From *The New Zealand
Tablet*, Dunedin.—"It may be read with profit not only by
Protestants but also by Catholics, whose liberality of mind
tends to degenerate into licence." From *The Western Catholic News*, Chicago (American).—"The book is an encyclopædia
of essential information on the subjects treated for either Protestants or Catholics." From *The Catholic News*, Preston.—
"That Father MacLaughlin has accomplished his task will be
patent to any one who reads the book." From *Freeman's
Journal*.—"It looks like gilding refined gold to say a word
as to the value of a book which has reached to a circulation
of fifteen thousand, and is still in the pleasant position of
being asked for as fresh.ly and as eagerly as ever." From
The Southern Cross, South Australia.—"The language and
style are perfect, and the spirit and tone which pervade temperate, just and fair." From *The Holy Family* (American),
New Orleans.—"We commend the work heartily to all."
From *The Manchester Guardian* (Non-Catholic).—"The author
writes with ability from the standpoint of the Church of Rome,
in the first place against 'Indifferentism," and in the second
to prove that his Church alone possesses the marks of unity
and universality." From *The Boston Pilot* (American).—
"This book bids fair to rival in popularity Father Lambert's
celebrated *Notes on Ingersoll*." From *The Irish Ecclesiastical
Record* (Monthly).—"Father MacLaughlin has done for 'Indifferentism'—by the way, why has he dropped this expressive
and highly appropriate title?—what Father Lambert, the author
of *Notes on Ingersoll* and the *Tactics of Infidels*, has done for
the scurrilous atheism of America. He has scotched if not
killed it, and has rendered it impossible for any one who has
read ever again to profess the belief that one religion is as
good as another." From *The Glasgow Herald* (Non-Catholic).

—" Mr. MacLaughlin writes clearly, and from his premises on the whole logically." From *The Dundee Advertiser* (Non-Catholic).—" The book is really worth reading." From *The North Wales Guardian*, Wrexham.—" From the beginning to the end it is full of plain, straightforward reasoning, and the arguments are stated clearly and forcibly. The author is evidently master of the situation." From *The Welshman*, Carmarthen.—" He certainly writes with uncommon ability, and is a very close reasoner. He confines himself a good deal to Scripture, and makes little use of patristic or mediæval writings." From *The Coventry Standard.*—" The writer (a Roman Catholic), the Rev. John MacLaughlin, has produced a book emphatically one for the times. The tone is earnest and kindly; it is free from bitterness, well seasoned, logical." From *The Bristol Observer.*—" There is much in the book which will claim and will have the sympathy of Protestants as well as Catholics. Mr. MacLaughlin puts his case forcibly throughout." From *The Monitor*, San Francisco.—" A most interesting and instructive volume of over 200 pages." From *The Glasgow Evening Times.*—" In an excellent style, simple and clear, and devoid of ornate trappings, lies the secret of Mr. MacLaughlin's success." From *The Glasgow Observer.*—" No Catholic book of controversy has ever been so favourably reviewed by the non-Catholic press." From *The National Press*, Dublin.—" He puts plain truths before his readers in the most convincing style that could be adopted." From *The Star*, London.—" His work on 'Indifferentism' has secured a circulation which for a religious work may be truly described as abnormal." From *The Sunday Tablet*, New York.—" Has done the work with singular ability and convincing logic." From *The Westmoreland Gazette*, Kendal.—" An exceedingly useful manual for the humble housewife who wishes to bring a wholesome, varied and palatable diet within the range of a very limited exchequer." From *The Newcastle Daily Chronicle*, Newcastle-upon-Tyne.—" A new edition of the powerful treatise by the Rev. John MacLaughlin. The work is written from a Catholic standpoint, but for the sake of its attack on 'Indifferent-ism' its circulation has been promoted by some not belonging to that persuasion." From *The Hampshire Independent*, Southampton.—" The writer claims as the *raison d'être* of the publication that the spirit of 'Indifferentism,' against which it is directed, is quite as injurious to strict Protestantism as it is to Roman Catholicism." From *The Halifax Mercury.*—" Is worthy of a thoughtful perusal. He selects his own starting-point, and with this privilege conceded reasons fairly and logically." From *The Faith of Our Fathers.*—" From first to last this book is one that should find its way into the hands of Protestants." From *The Catholic Mirror.*—" This treatise, we may say without hyperbole, possesses all the characteristics by which such a work should be distinguished." From *The Caxton Review.*—" Has passed unscathed under the batteries of the press, both Catholic and non-Catholic." From *The Northampton Herald.*—" The writer has honourably fulfilled his self-imposed task." From *The Leicester Chronicle and Leicestershire Mercury.*—" This is a useful contribution to the discussion from the point of view of a Roman Catholic priest." From *The Bookseller.*—" . . . Well deserves the high praise bestowed upon it by its most anti-Roman critics." From *The East Anglian Daily Times.*—" The writer, the Rev. John Mac-Laughlin, has penned something worthy of consideration."